Veronica Brady in Her Own Words

Veronica Brady in Her Own Words

Adelaide
2021

A Forum for Theology in the World
Volume 8, Issue 1 & 2, 2021

A Forum for Theology in the World is an academic refereed journal aimed at engaging with issues in the contemporary world, a world which is pluralist and ecumenical in nature. The journal reflects this pluralism and ecumenism. Each edition is theme specific and has its own editor responsible for the production. The journal aims to elicit and encourage dialogue on topics and issues in contemporary society and within a variety of religious traditions. The Editor in Chief welcomes submissions of manuscripts, collections of articles, for review from individuals or institutions, which may be from seminars or conferences or written specifically for the journal. An internal peer review is expected before submitting the manuscript. It is the expectation of the publisher that, once a manuscript has been accepted for publication, it will be submitted according to the ATF Press house style which will be supplied by the publisher.

All submissions to the Editor in Chief are to be sent to: hdregan@atf.org.au.

Each edition is available as a journal subscription, or as a book in print, pdf or epub, through the ATF Press web site — www.atfpress.com. Journal subscriptions are also available through EBSCO and other library suppliers.

Editor in Chief
Hilary Regan, ATF Press

A Forum for Theology in the World is published by ATF Theology and imprint of
ATF (Australia) Ltd (ABN 90 116 359 963) and
is published twice or three times a year.

ISBN: 978-1-922737-41-0 Soft
          978-1-922737-42-7 Hard
          978-1-922737-43-4 Epub
          978-1-922737-44-1 Pdf

Published and edited by

THEOLOGY

Making a lasting impact

An imprint of the ATF Press Publishing Group
owned by ATF (Australia) Ltd.
PO Box 234
Brompton, SA 5007
Australia
ABN 90 116 359 963
www.atfpress.com

Table of Contents

A Forum for Theology in the World Vol 8 No 1&2/2021

Introducing Key Themes in Her Writings

We live in difficult, some would even say ugly times. Moreover, religion can often seem part of that ugliness. But if that is so, it is important to reflect on what we mean by 'religion' and then what we mean by 'beauty'. Both are slippery words, hard to define since they have to do with individual experience. The Maquarie Dictionary's definition of religion as 'the quest for the values of the ideal life', however, establishes common ground between them since beauty also offers a glimpse of that life. In what I have to say I want to explore these connections, looking at the evidence in life and literature.

Veronica Brady, 1929–2015

'God is Dead, anyway.
Anyway—Thank God—In Australia.'
The Workings Of God In A Secular Society

The quotation with which we begin, from Patrick White's *The Vivisector*, points to the paradox I want to explore, the ways in which God, 'the unacknowledged factor', may continue to work in a secular society like Australia in which, as the quotation suggests, that factor is largely disregarded. The conversation which provides my title is between two fashionable people at a retrospective exhibition of the work of White's fictional painter Hurtle Duffield and their opinions are typical enough. But if we take Charles Taylor's point about the importance of symbolic expression for deciphering what may be otherwise inexpressible in a secular culture like ours, it is worth noting that the life of Duffield, the novel's protagonist turns on his quest for and attempt to paint God, 'the otherwise unnameable I-N-D-I-G-O'[1]—indigo being the ultimate colour in the alchemical spectrum—and that he dies in a final attempt to do so. The novel is thus suggesting first, that the word 'God' means little or nothing to many, perhaps most Australians, and secondly that what it refers to is beyond words, as Jean-Luc Marion puts it, *'hors-texte'* ('without being')[2] but so important that it is worth dying for.

I want to begin by arguing, paradoxically perhaps, that the apparent disbelief in God may not be as negative as it sounds, at least if we accept that religion which the Macquarie Dictionary defines as a 'a particular system in which the quest for the ideal life has been embodied' is not necessarily the same as faith, a personal 'commitment to realities at present unseen' (Heb 11:1). Many cultures, however,

---

1. Patrick White, *The Vivisector* (London: Cape, 1970), 641.
2. Jean-Luc Marion, *God Without Being* (London, University of Chicago Press, 1991).

tend to see the two as synonymous, which often means that religion replaces faith—as Marx (following Feuerbach) pointed out, what many people call God is a projection of emotional, social, economic or political need.[3] So the fact that our culture is officially secular may leave more room for the living God, the God beyond words, whose best definition may, as JB Metz suggests, be 'interruption'. But before we go any further we need to reflect further on the kind of society in which we find ourselves.

It is a settler society, one in which in contrast to traditional societies the self's primary question tends to be 'what world can I possess?' rather than 'where do I belong in the scheme of things?' Ours is also the product of British imperial history which tended to be less concerned than the earlier empires of Spain and Portugal with spreading the Gospel than with economics and politics, specifically in our case with relieving the pressure on Britain's overcrowded prisons and establishing a base for trade in the Pacific. For these reasons our beginnings were not particularly gracious. The arrival of the First Fleet was less monumental than orgiastic, for instance, and for some time might was often more important than right—indeed some would suggest that this is still the case.

In this situation the civil religion the Establishment brought with them functioned as a more or less optional extra while for the Irish, many of them convicts or struggling settlers, the Holy Roman Empire represented their answer to the British Empire. But this could be seen as an opportunity for the God who exists outside the text of history, though he/she also intervenes in it. As Ian Turner observed:

> A religion which was appropriate for the ordered society and regular living of rural England seemed irrelevant to pioneering labour in the Australian bush. Men carved their own lives out of a remote and monstrously difficult wilderness; what they achieved they owed to themselves, and they found little for which to thank their fathers' heaven.[4]

Nevertheless for those of us who believe in the God whose 'being is in coming . . . [who] goes on ways to himself, even when they lead to

---

3. Lloyd Easton and Kurt Guddat, editors, *Writings Of The Young Marx On Philosophy And Society* (New Yok, Doubleday Anchor Book, 1967), 250.
4. Ian Turner, *The Australian Dream* (Melbourne, Sun Books, 1968), x.

other places, even to that which is not God', ways which can 'include something like distance from himself too',[5] what someone has called a 'God-shaped hole' must exist even here.

As Charles Taylor suggests, this hole is often apparent in literature and the arts generally. So let us return to Patrick White, to a passage from another novel, *The Solid Mandala,* a conversation this time between Arthur Brown, a young man who is seen, especially by his intellectually pretentious twin brother as a 'dill' and his pious but well-meaning neighbour Mrs Poulter who asks Arthur why none of his family ever went to church, to which he replies that they "'began to feel it wasn't true.'" This shocks her and she tells him that she "'couldn't exist without Our Lord.'" His response, however, echoes Marx's critique of mere religion asking: "'Could He exist without *you?*'" He has no time for pious statements, knowing from experience that many "'Christians are cruel'", ready to "'crucify'" people like him who are different.[6] Later, however, he dances out for her his vision of God as the crucified one, involved in our pain. Eventually, after his death, Mrs Poulter understands what he has been saying, as catching a glimpse of the sufferings of the wars and violence of our times as the 'God' of her complacencies 'fell down, in a thwack of canvas, a cloud of dust'.[7] This is a theme which runs like a refrain through White's work, that 'Man is not God' and that, as 'our fevers for power' make us think, but also that God shows himself often as 'Man with a spear in his side'.[8]

This suggests that the suspicion of organised religion, apparent in our culture, though somewhat diminished today by the growth of fundamentalism, may have theological significance. One of the founding figures of the 'Australian tradition' in our literature, Joseph Furphy, for instance, rejected what he called the 'phylactered exclusivism', seeing 'ecclesiastical Christianity . . . as a failure of the first magnitude, since it had of ecclesiastical made the cross, 'the symbol of deepest ignominy . . . the proudest insignia of Court-moths and professional assassins'.[9] For him God 'is by his own authority

5. Eberhard Jüngel, *God As The Mystery of The World,* translated by Darrell Guder (Grand Rapids, MI: Eerdmans, 1983), 159.

6. Patrick White, *The Solid Mandala* (London: Eyre & Spottiswoode, 1966), 261–262.

7. White, *The Solid Mandala,* 303.

8. White, *The Vivisector,* 296–297.

9. John Barnes, editor, *Portable Australian Authors: Joseph Furphy* (St Lucia: University of Queensland Press, 1981), 89–90.

represented by the poorest of the poor'.[10] In this respect the tradition of the 'fair go', the belief that in words of seventeenth century Christian John Lilburne, 'the poorest he hath as much right as the richest he and demands our respect and care, has religious significance.

Yet it does not really address what I see as the central question which is both ontological and epistemological, the question of authority, whether or not there is a reality beyond human history to which we owe obedience. By definition, as we have said our society is the product of imperial history, but a history which was in the nineteenth century fuelled by the neo-Darwinism which replaced belief in God with belief in historical inevitability, in the evolutionary struggle of all against all in which the fittest—people like us—were destined to triumph and thus made the imperial self 'the basis and referent of the whole of reality spread out at its feet',[11] locking us in a 'closed circle around sameness',[12] with disastrous consequences for the land's First Peoples but also for the land and its flora and fauna.

If we return to the belief that God continues to go on ways to Godself through this world and also that this God may manifest himself as the crucified, then it appears that God may be speaking to us in these wounded ones, calling us out of our closed circle to recognise the claims of the other/Other upon us. This is our crucial opportunity since, as Emmanuel Levinas argues, it 'is in the laying down by the ego of its sovereignty [in this way] . . . that we find ethics and also probably the very spirituality of the soul, but most certainly the question of the meaning of being.'[13] The recognition the environmental crisis is urging on us is challenging the arrogance of our exploitative culture in this way and it can thus be seen as an occasion of grace. But my time is running out, leaving no time to explore this insight. Instead let me conclude with a brief reflection on the significance for us of Aboriginal Australia.

The Biblical figure of the Suffering Servant, I suggest, is important here. 'Despised and rejected by others; a man of suffering acquainted with infirmity' who has in fact been 'wounded for our transgressions, crushed for our iniquities', this figure is nevertheless the one 'through him [that] the will of the Lord shall prosper' (Isa 55:3, 5, 10). This is

---

10. Barnes, *Portable Australian Authors*, 86.

11. Luiz Carlos Susin, 'A Critique Of The Identity Paradigm', in *Concilium*, 2 (2000): 80.

12. Susin, 'A Critique Of The Identity Paradigm', 87.

13. Sean Hand, editor, *The Levinas Reader* (Oxford: Blackwell, 1993), 85.

because in contemplating his fate we may understand who we really are before God but also what we must do if we are to realise his will for us. It thus calls us to renounce our allegiance to the dynamisms of contemporary history and give our allegiance to his logic according to which the true meaning of human history may lie with the 'losers' rather than the 'winners' and that, as Walter Benjamin puts it: 'Victory bears its fruits entirely differently from the way in which defeat has its consequences.'[14]

These fruits are theological. Although they are at a discount in a secular age, it is our task to accept that this is so and to live out the consequences. In the long run, I would argue, it is they which will enable us to survive.

---

14. Bam Mertens, 'Benjamin: "Hope, Yes, But Not For Us": Messianism and Redemption In The Work Of Walter Benjamin', in Wayne Cristaudo and Wendy Baker, editors, *Messianism Apocalypse & Redemption In 20th Century German Thought* (Adelaide: ATF Press, 2006), 76.

'Keep Your Mind In Hell And Despair Not.' *For The Term Of His Natural Life* And The Possibilities of Isolation

It may seem odd to reflect on a novel about isolation of the most extreme kind, the hell of the convict system in Van Diemen's Land, and to gain from it an insight into connection, a deeper notion of community. But that, I suggest, is the possibility hinted at in the words of a Russian thinker Staretz Siloman which I have taken for my epigraph. As he sees it, existence is robbed of its weight and gravity when it is deprived of its *agon*. Walter Benjamin made a similar point when, reflecting on the meaning of history in general on what he called 'the tradition of the oppressed' in particular, he wrote that although the vanquished may have lost in war they did not lose their history. For them it is true, 'those events are truly finished and lost to their *praxis* . . . Victory bears its fruits entirely differently from the way in which defeat has its consequences.'[1] Nevertheless, he argues, past suffering lays another claim on the present and this is the claim I would like to explore in Marcus Clarke's novel about this system, *For The Term Of His Natural Life* which was itself a work of historical remembrance since it was written after the system had ended.

Remembrance, as Benjamin also points out, can modify what the events themselves seemed to have determined. Hannah Arendt writes in similar vein when she remarks that human society began with crime. 'Whatever brotherhood human beings may be capable of has grown out of fratricide, whatever political organisation men

---

1. Bram Mertens, '"Hope, Yes, But Not For Us" Messianism And Redemption In The Work Of Walter Benjamin', in Wayne Cristaudo & Wendy Baker, editors *Messianism Apocalypse & Redemption In 20ᵗʰ Century German Thought* (Adelaide: ATF Press, 2006), 76.

may have achieved has its origins in crime',[2] in injustice particularly. Certainly non-Aboriginal Australia had such a beginning. But from it, I suggest, there developed a search for a different kind of community, the kind, I suggest, articulated, however awkwardly, at the end of the nineteenth century in the ideal of a 'fair go' for all and the notion of 'mateship', though in recent times it has fallen into abeyance, perhaps because of a relentless focus on the future at the expense of a more troubling past which, to anticipate a central point to be made later, has lead to the neglect of an essential, if often unprofessed factor in the formation of authentic community, what Benjamin calls the 'theological', the 'refusal to accept the finality of past suffering' and the determination to redeem it.[3]

For The Term Of His Natural Life, as we have said is a work of this kind of Remembrance, the more powerful. I think, because it is a work of fiction and thus able to explore possibilities beyond rational comprehension and otherwise unspeakable since they belong to the realm the of unconscious, 'the archaic, the nocturnal and the oneiric'[4] which nevertheless often shapes events and people more deeply than we realise. That is why in my discussion of Clarke's novel I want first of all to refer to a passage in another work about imprisonment, Primo Levi's *If This Is A Man*,[5] an account of his experience as a prisoner in a Nazi concentration camp, a passage which points in this direction and in doing so illuminates the theme of community which runs through *For The Term Of His Natural Life*.

Both works, as we have said, are about imprisonment and both insist on the isolation of a situation in each man exists alone in a world in which human community has all but disappeared, a world ruled by force without the moderating influence of law which is in this sense worse than Dante's hell (which is central to the passage from Levi's book) which was at least governed by a certain proportion between the crime committed and its punishment. This was not so in the Nazi camps or in Clarke's novel: Dawes, the central character, is

---

2. Hannah Arendt, *On Revolution* (Ringwood: Penguin, 1973), 20.
3. See Mertens, "'Hope, Yes, But Not For Us'".
4. Marcus Clarke, *For The Term Of His Natural Life* (Sydney: AR Classics, 2002), 240. All page references hereafter will be given in my text.
5. I will be using the French translation of the Italian *Se Questo E Un Uomo, Si C'est Un Homme* (Paris: Julliard, 1987). The translation into English is mine and all page references will be given in my text.

in fact an innocent man who is being punished for another's crime. In both places therefore authority was brutal or stupid or complacent, 'virtue a mere name' and existence (in Levi's words) 'a bible of pain' (83) subjecting them to degrading labour and brutal punishment for the slightest infractions. There was no comfort even from the natural world. Levi's account is full of the torments of winter's cold and Clarke describes Van Diemen's Land as a savage and unfamiliar place on the other side of the world whose coast, lashed by howling winds and cold, looked like 'a biscuit at which rats have been nibbling' (97). How then did the shape of a different kind of community emerge from these appalling beginnings?

This is where what I take to be the central passage in Levi's work is illuminating. It comes towards the end of his time in the camp. It is mid winter and he and a fellow prisoner, like him 'engaged in a personal and secret battle against the camp and death' (143), are carrying the bucket of soup which is their ration from the kitchen to the hut they occupy with their fellow prisoners when a scene from Dante's *Divine Comedy* suddenly comes to mind, the scene in the depths of hell, in Canto XXVI of the *Inferno* in which the poet and Virgil, his guide, meet the Greek hero Ulysses. It is a poignant moment as Ulysses recalls the moment after several attempts when he and his crew finally sailed through the Pillars of Hercules out of the Mediterranean into the open sea beyond. The description of the mountain they see on shore just before they are overwhelmed by a sudden whirlwind reminds Levi of the mountain near his home when he, too, was a free man.

According to most commentators this is a crucial moment in Dante's journey. Like Ulysses he has longed to 'experience . . . that which lies beyond/ the sun, and . . . the world that is unpeopled'. But he is in hell for this reason. He has overreached himself and is being punished for sacrilege, for defying the fact that human beings are not autonomous but belong to a cosmic order whose laws they must obey. This is not the way we imagine things today. For us the individual is free, sometimes almost obliged, to realise his/her desires wherever they may lead. But recalling this passage in the mindless, soulless vacuum of the camp, Levi is suddenly nostalgic for Dante's vision which now seems 'so human, so necessary and so neglected', presupposing as it does a 'gigantic reality' beyond the self 'which perhaps contains the explanation of our destiny and our presence here' (151) and for this reason should 'concern everyone who suffers' (149) since we are all responsible for and to one another. Defying this reality the Nazis have created the hell in which he finds himself.

This sense that this community of mutual responsibility and respect is essential for a proper humanity is also, I suggest, the central point that Clarke's novel makes, even if here only three people, Dawes, Sylvia, the daughter of the commandant of the settlement, and North, one of the two chaplains, achieve it. Dawes is the first to catch a glimpse of it, though it is Sylvia, at this stage a mere child, who shows it to him. Significantly, however, it is not revealed in words but in an event which challenges the system which imprisons him by suggesting that a different order is possible, one based not on brute force but on compassion and respect.

Dawes has just managed to escape from solitary confinement on an island off the larger penal settlement of Sarah Island when he stumbles on survivors of the ship wrecked taking Sylvia away from the settlement under the escort of the officer Maurice Frere. On the run and half starved, he is a frightening figure and Frere responds aggressively. But the child Sylvia, moved by compassion for him, offers him some of their dwindling supply of food. This is a turning point for Dawes. The inscription over the gates of Dante's Hell read 'Abandon hope, all you who enter here.' But Sylvia's gesture tells him that goodness still exists and kindles the hope that he may yet belong again to the community of human beings. According to Theodor Adorno, this kind of hope is 'the only philosophy which can be responsibly practised in the face of despair' since it involves an 'attempt to contemplate all things as they would present themselves from the standpoint of redemption' and thus resists current reality by negating it.[6]

The word 'redemption' here, of course, has theological overtones and may therefore seem unfashionable. But if we define theology as Martin Marty does as a 'mode of awareness that evokes a transcendence of other transcendences . . . [by prompting] a way of attending to human experience from a perspective beyond our life world'[7] the impact Sylvia's gesture makes on Dawes is theological. It also liberates him from his isolation, from 'the dismal hermitage of his

6. David Kaufmann, 'In The Light Of "The Light of Transcendence": Redemption In Adorno', in Cristaudo & Baker, 36.

7. Jack Hill, 'Images Of Religion In South Pacific Fiction: An Interpretation Of *Pouliuli*', in *Literature And Theology*, 17/2 (June 2003): 187.

mind' (128) so that he regains the 'air of independence and authority' (178) which had been his when he was a free man and becomes an active and effective member of this small community of castaways. In fact he proves himself a better man than Frere—in this situation rank counts for nothing—by guiding the party back to the settlement, but at his own expense. Once there the system takes over. Frere regains his authority, lies about Dawes' behaviour and all the credit for their rescue and Dawes is returned to captivity and punished for his escape.

Implicitly a contrast is drawn here between two different kinds of community, what Augustine calls the 'City of Man' which is based on love of self at the expense of the other—the community to which Frere subscribes—and the 'City of God' which Dawes has discovered, based on love of the other at the expense of the self. In passing it is worth noting that this distinction may suggest that what we see as our present 'era of increased connectivity' may be moving in the opposite direction, to the extent that in it there are signs of increasing exploitation of and disconnection with the other. If this is so it is worth exploring the kind of community which Dawes glimpsed as Levi did even in the hell in which he found himself. This is especially the case, I would argue, if the tradition of a 'fair go', that is of this kind of community, which developed in this country may have derived from similar beginnings in reaction to the convict system.

Essentially this community does not rely on institutions or on the power of the state but originates from below, in what Walter Benjamin calls 'the tradition of the oppressed,'[8] from the hope for a better world. In *For The Term Of His Natural Life* the third member of this kind of community is an unexpected figure, the clergyman North who is supposedly an Establishment figure. In contrast with the other chaplain, the obsequious Meekin, he is appalled by the injustices of the system and protests against them, perhaps because he himself is acquainted with suffering, being a secret alcoholic. But distanced in this way from 'decent society' enables him to 'see around the corner where a different, unfamiliar life [is] . . . going on,'[9] helping him to take his beliefs as a Christian seriously rather than merely socially as Meekin does—and here Clarke may be giving a positive twist to Nietzsche's proposition that Christianity is the religion of slaves.

8. Mertens, "'Hope, Yes, But Not For Us", in Cristaudo & Baker, 74.
9. Frances Day, 'The Fate Of Hope In Hollow Spaces: Ernst Bloch's Messianism', in Cristaudo & Baker, 41

North's protests against the system reach a climax when a young convict, Kirkland, is flogged to death and he goes to the commandant to demand an inquiry. The commandant, Sylvia's father, is basically decent. But he is a servant of the system. So, like the Germans Hannah Arendt describes who went along with Hitler, resisting the 'temptation of doing good',[10] he refuses on the grounds that an inquiry would take too long and cost too much. In reply North appeals to the 'concept of something that would differ from the unspeakable world that is',[11] the belief that every human being is absolutely valuable and that we are all responsible for one another, telling the commandant that '[n]o trouble, no expense, no dissatisfaction, should stand in the way of humanity and justice' (331).

His vehemence, however, is partly fuelled by self-disgust since at the time of the flogging he was too drunk to attend—as he should have done—and this disgust is increased by the behaviour of Dawes, ordered to flog the boy who refuses half-way to continue and is himself savagely punished as a consequence. So when he hears this North goes to see him in his solitary confinement, confesses his failure and asks the convict to forgive him. At this moment Dawes glimpses 'a misery more profound than his own' (328) but also once more realises, as he did in Sylvia's gesture years before, that goodness still exists. A bond grows up between them and North visits him again. Dawes tells him how he came to be here, that he has been convicted for a murder he did not commit. Listening to his story, North realises that he is responsible since he had arrived on the murder scene first but instead of pursuing the murderer had had made off with the dead man's wallet, needing money to pay off his gambling debts, leaving Dawes who arrived shortly afterwards to be arrested for the murder. To add to his pain he realises that North is in love with Sylvie, now a grown woman and unhappily married to Frere—as he is also.

In realistic terms these coincidences are not easy to accept. But as far as our argument is concerned they create a community of mutual respect between the two men and for North a sense of responsibility for the sufferings of the other. He decides therefore to make reparation, to have Dawes take his place on the ship which

---

10. Hannah Arendt, *Eichmann In Jerusalem: A Report On The Banality Of Evil* (Camberwell Vic: Penguin, 1994), 150.

11. Kaufmann, 'In The Light Of "The Light of Transcendence"', in Cristaudo & Baker, 41.

is also about to take Sylvia away. To refer to Benjamin once again, he argues that North's situation here can only be properly resolved in what he calls 'theological' terms which make it possible for guilt to lead to 'grace, redemption and sacrifice'.[12] By leaving the door of Dawes' cell open when he leaves and leaving his own cloak behind for Dawes to use so that the boatman will mistake Dawes for himself North sacrifices his own freedom and position.

As it happens the ship sinks in a cyclone which suddenly overwhelms it and Dawes and Sylvia are drowned. But this, it could be said, points to the insight that the kind of community envisaged here demands a radical break with the world it describes, pointing as it does to possibilities as yet unrealised. The description of the last moments of Sylvia and Dawes, I think, suggests a 'transvaluation of value' of this kind: 'In the great crisis of our life, when, brought face to face with annihilation, we are suspended gasping over the great emptiness of death, we become conscious that the Self we thought we knew so well has strange and unthought of capacities' (537).

The language and tenor here may not be fashionable, But it makes a point worth reflection, Benjamin's point, that the consequences of defeat are different from the fruits of victory and that the 'losers' may have a meaning yet to be realised and that this meaning may need to be reworked by remembrance. At the very least it returns us to Adorno's argument that the only knowledge that can be responsibly practised in the face of despair is one which offers hope of redemption, and thus 'interrogates the world as it is, revealing it to be . . . as indigent and as distorted at it will appear one day'[13]—if we continue to contest it. It also underlines the fact that the kind of alternative community represented by Dawes, Sylvia and North may be central to that hope.

This may seem utopian. But Benjamin's reflections on history especially his discussion of the ideology of 'progress'—central, of course, to the culture of consumption, growth and technological efficiency—suggest that it is not. He sees it as a storm which is relentlessly driving us into a future over which we have no control 'while the mountain of devastation before [our] eyes grows to high heaven.' But the Angel of History's

---

12. Mertens, "'Hope, Yes, But Not For Us", in Cristaudo & Baker, 63.
13. Kaufman, 'In The Light Of "The Light of Transcendence"', in Cristaudo & Baker, 36.

face is turned towards the past. Where *we* see a chain of events, *he* sees one single catastrophe, which incessantly heaps ruin upon ruin and slings them in front of his feet. He would like to resist the storm to stay, to wake the dead and to restore what has been torn asunder.[14]

But that restoration, Benjamin suggests, depends upon the rediscovery of the 'theological'. The dimension to do with being rather than having (which rules our present culture) which he represents as the dwarf in the chess machine of history, a reality 'which is small and ugly nowadays, and cannot show itself under any circumstances' but which nevertheless in his view 'animates and manipulates the outward machinery which represents historical materialism'[15] since it points beyond it to the 'quest for happiness of a free humanity.[16]

To conclude then. I have been arguing that *For The Term Of His Natural Life* makes a similar point, challenging the convict system's culture of disconnection, implying instead that in the long run a human community properly rests on concern for rather than exploitation of the other. As Emmanuel Levinas argues, a society which 'wipes out all otherness by murder or by all-encompassing and totalising thought . . . or war and politics' is ultimately unsustainable since it is 'only in the laying down by the ego of its sovereignty (in its 'hateful' modality), that we find ethics and . . . the meaning of being, that is, its appeal for justification.'[17] To reflect on the past, on the convict system in Van Diemen's Land or on the Nazi prison camps, on those apparently defeated by history, may therefore be important for any discussion of the good society.

---

14. Mertens, '"Hope, Yes, But Not For Us", in Cristaudo & Baker, 73.
15. Mertens, '"Hope, Yes, But Not For Us", in Cristaudo & Baker, 76.
16. Mertens, '"Hope, Yes, But Not For Us", in Cristaudo & Baker, 69.
17. Sean Hand, editor, *The Levinas Reader* (Oxford: Blackwell, 1993), 85.

'Not God, But Life, A Larger, Richer, More Satisfying Life': Lightening The Fire And Keeping It Burning

---

These words from William James' classic *Varieties Of Religious Experience*, I believe, sum up the challenge facing religious educators, reminding us that, properly understood, religion is not a matter of intellectual or moral propositions but opens a way to this larger life, the experience of some ultimate 'is-ness' beyond our human understanding which is nevertheless revealed to us in our most intense experiences and is thus, paradoxically, profoundly intimate since, as James goes on to say, it has to do with 'eaches' not 'alls', though we can also and often do experience it in our everyday ordinary lives.

It follows we should think of religion not just as another 'subject', like 'subject', like mathematics or geography, but a way of being, a form of wisdom rather than of mere knowledge—at least if we define wisdom in its original sense which derives from two Anglo-Saxon words; 'wys' the equivalent of the Greek word 'arete', the perfection of a person, animal or thing, and '-domit' an abiding state, and Levinas implied a similar understanding when he defined a 'wise' person as someone aware of 'a new plot in being above the human and the animal', living a 'true life' which he saw as one in tune with 'the normative idealism of what must be'[1] a definition which echoes the Biblical definition of faith as commitment to 'realities at present unseen' (Heb 11:1).

These, I believe, are the realities we need to explore, live by and cherish as educators and share with others. But this is a task which demands patience, faithfulness and attentiveness, none of which is particularly attractive in the culture of instant gratification we inhabit.

---

1. This the title of one of his majors works: Jean Luc Marion, *God Without Being* (London: Chicago University Press 1995).

So for many our contemporaries religion is merely 'pie in the sky', irrelevant to what DH Lawrence described as the central business of our culture, the 'business of money-making, money-having and money-spending'. At the other end of the scale Marx dismissed it as the 'opium of the people', a confidence trick, the product of emotional and intellectual cowardice and the desire for comfort and security— neither of which is likely to appeal to most young people today.

In fact, however, this is not the God revealed in the Judeo-Christian tradition who is very different; dynamic and explosive and not merely static, a God whose existence is beyond any human understanding, 'beyond and without being', as Eberhard Jüngel puts it.[2] So for Karl Barth, the words, institutions and rituals through and in which we attempt to speak about divine reality can ultimately be no more than craters caused by God's explosion into his creation or, to use another image, to a river flowing through it which—as rivers often do— changes course from time to time, with the result that some people who regard themselves a believers may in fact be sitting on the banks of a river which has flowed elsewhere.

By definition, as we have said, God exists beyond any category our minds can comprehend, cannot be possessed, but rather possesses all things and all people and is other than anything we can know or imagine, the *'mysterium tremendum et fascinans'* figured, for example, in Exodus as the bush burning in the dessert which is never consumed, but supremely in the broken and humiliated body on the Cross. According to JB Metz therefore, the best short way of speaking about God is perhaps summed up by the word 'interruption', an experience which breaks into, gives a sense of discontinuity to our everyday expectations. But God's interruption is not momentary but in a sense continuous, if we accept Eberhard Jüngel's proposition that God's 'being is in coming' in 'going on ways to himself through through this world' even when these ways 'lead to other places, even to that which is not God.'

This is a complicated process, however, since as Jüngel goes on to argue, 'thinking God 'means being 'taken along by God',[3] a process which Emmanuel Levinas suggests, usually originates in 'gropings to

---

2. Eberhard Jüngel, *God as the Mystery of the World* (Grand Rapids: Eerdman, 1981), 171.
3. Jüngel, *God as the Mystery of the World,* 169.

which one does not even know how to give verbal form, initial shocks [which] become questions and problems'.[4] For most young people, however, this is familiar territory, which suggests that it may be a more effective place at which to begin discussing belief in God than the more propositional approach of traditional catechetics.

True, experience, especially experience of this kind, can be difficult to express and can easily become messy and difficult to control and talk about. Nevertheless, it is in the province of the arts in general and in literature in particular it becomes more or less explicit, though in oblique ways. So let us consider Tim Winton's recent novel *Breath*, the story of two boys growing up in a small mill town in the timber country not far from the ocean in the south west of Western Australia and of their longings to escape from the boredom in a place in which 'men did solid, practical things' by doing 'something beautiful. Something pointless and elegant, as though nobody saw or cared'.[5]

The narrator is the main character, Bruce Pike ('Pikelet' to his friend Loonie) as an older man, who has become an ambulance officer, looking back on their attempts to escape from boredom into a life, which 'pointless and elegant, as though nobody saw or cared' (23). Pikelet's parents, English migrants, determined to protect him, have forbidden him to go near the ocean since his father once saw a fisherman swept off the rocks by a huge wave and smashed against the cliffs.

They are also troubled by his friendship with Loonie, the town 'tear-away', whose mother has walked out on them, and his father, the local publican, consoles himself with other women, so leaving the boy free to do whatever he likes. For the two boys the town is a place of sheer boredom, a trap which 'renders you powerless by dragging you back to it, breath upon breath in an endless capitulation to biological routine' (41). The 'non-negotiable secularity' of the 'bare plains and dark forests' of the surrounding countryside is equally boring so that 'time and meaning have hardened into a kind of leaden meaninglessness'.[6]

---

4. *Ethics And Infinity: Conversations With Philippe Nemo* (Pittsburg: Duquesne University Press, 2003), 20–21
5. Tim Winton, *Breath* (Camberwell, Vic: Hamish Hamilton/Penguin Books, 2008), 23. Hereafter all page references will be given in the text of the essay.
6. Charles Taylor, *A Secular Age* (London: Harvard University Press, 2007), 715.

So for them, in rebellion even 'against the monotony of drawing breath', God is 'barely possible'. And the only elsewhere is 'America', land of 'mighty canyons . . . mile-wide rivers . . . and] soaring peaks and snow' (137). To pass the time Loonie devises a game which involves gambling with death; diving into the local swimming hole in the river, staying underwater as long as they can and then surfacing to enjoy the alarm they have caused. But soon that also becomes boring. So he turns to surfing. At first, obedient to his parents, Pikelet does not join him. Then one day, out on his bike, he catches his first glimpse of the ocean and is overwhelmed by its grandeur:

> From the great granite headland whose rocks were daubed with warnings about the dangerous current, the beach stretched east for miles. We watched the surfers plunge into the churning rip alongside the rocks and from there they shot toward the break. Waves ground around the headland, line upon line of them, smooth and turquoise, reeling across the bay to spend themselves in a final mauling rush against the bar at the river mouth. The air seethed with noise and salt: I was giddy with it (22).

The glimpse of its power fascinates him and he longs also to do something like this, 'pointless and elegant, as though nobody saw or cared' (23). As his mentor, Sando, later says to him 'It's not even about us . . . It's about you. You and the sea. You and the planet' (75), feeling 'the hand of God' (76). But for the time being Pikelet obeys his parents, watching enviously as Sando plunges into 'a different life, another society, a state for which no raw boy has either words or experience to describe. But, as Charles Taylor points out, 'the social imaginary' even of the very ordinary world he lives in, enframed as it is by a 'deeply entrenched if implicit common understanding of structure and counter-structure' is also 'capable of being taken up by a host of different moral vectors' and becoming 'wildly destructive'.[7]

When Pikelet meets Sando and his girl friend Eva everything changes. He begins to surf in the most dangerous place and has his first sexual adventures with Eva. As for Loonie, his life becomes more and more excessive as he pursues obsession with terror and danger across the world and dies eventually in a bar in Mexico, killed as a result of a drug deal gone wrong.

---

7. Charles Taylor, *A Secular Age*, 715.

This is the kind of story, I suggest, to interest most young people. But this perhaps is the crisis point of adolescence, the experience of the sacred. But how to avoid being consumed by it? How to channel it into everyday life? I suggest it is important to realize it isn't God.

It is dangerous but demanded to be our task is to help young people catch a glimpse of this plot and learn ways of involving themselves in it, not merely intellectually but also existentially, and not merely as an optional extra but as their life's task. For most young people, I think, the fire of this faith is still burning. But all too often the religious forms and language they are offered tend to extinguish it, so that they look elsewhere. Tim Winton's latest novel *Breath*, I will argue, is about this search. By exploring it I hope to suggest ways of understanding its religious implications and thus creating the kind of school community and curriculum which will keep the fire burning not only in the present but for the future.

A Forum for Theology in the World Vol 8 No 1&2/2021

'Such is Life, My Fellow Mummers' . . . The Seditious Joseph Furphy

Words, as Joseph Furphy has Tom Collins saying, are tricky things, as slippery as wet melon seeds when you try to pick them up. So the current attempts to define 'Australian values' tend to be rather bemusing and in the long run lead me at least to conclude that the phrase, like the word beauty, points to something which largely exists in the eye of the beholder. Unfortunately, that does not prevent them being used, especially by politicians to paint those who disagree with them as suspect, even guilty of sedition, a word which has a fairly clear meaning, probably because it has legal and political origins, being defined as incitement of discontent or rebellion against government.

But those origins go back to the days of absolute monarchy and to the rulers intent on preserving absolute power. Most of us would like to think, however, that that is not the kind of government we have today, that we live in a democracy—an even more slippery word, of course but one that implies diversity and debate as people work at building community together under the umbrella of a set of values which include respect for individuals and for their beliefs and opinions and for the right to dissent and ask questions about the decisions of power. To come to the question at issue, sedition, if questioning the status quo and being in disagreement with certain governmental policies is seen as seditious then that in fact can be seen as an important element in the history of 'Australian values' and the current trend to use the term 'un-Australian' to enforce conformity as dangerously totalitarian in its implications.

In my more optimistic moments, however, I like to think that this kind of behaviour is not because this government has totalitarian tendencies but because its leaders have little sense of history, of the real—as distinct from a romanticised story of ordinary people, those our Prime Minister likes to call the 'battlers', since we arrived in this country and even less of the history of First Peoples who have lived here from time immemorial.

Instead, they live in the instantaneous present addicted to what DH Lawrence called the 'business of money-making, money-having and money-spending', bemused by fantasies of endless material expansion and consumption. The reality of the past is 'another country' so that those who believe we may have something to learn from it are suspect.

Exploring it, however, may contribute to the current discussion of 'Australian values' and help us understand better what the phrase implies. One way of doing this is by looking at imaginative evidence from the past since it can give a sense of the ways in which we have come to understand ourselves and our place in the world. One such piece of evidence is one which the literal minded and those with no time for jokes—the majority, I suspect, of those in positions of power—would probably regard as profoundly seditious and probably frivolous. Its author described it as not just 'a collection of lies, but one long involved lie, in 7 chapters'[1] and boasted of its 'outspoken contempt of fetish . . . calm Australian sufficiency, and . . . disregard of hostile opinion'[2] as it pursues its self-ironic way. That work is Joseph Furphy's *Such Is Life*, one of the seminal texts of what used to be called 'the Australian tradition.'

Its opening sentence, 'Unemployed at last!'[3] should upset those concerned to deal severely with 'dole bludgers' and 'welfare cheats'—though in defence of the offender, Furphy's narrator Tom Collins, it has to be said that he did then begin to write a book. Nevertheless there is no sense that work is the basis of citizenship and the only proper occupation for human beings: his characters spend most of their time talking, yarning to one another about the meaning of life in general and stories of good and bad luck in particular. It also mocks the narrow pragmatic and utilitarian premises of our culture, proclaiming in pseudo-heroic mode that Tom's unemployment is not the result of social but of cosmic causes but that 'the momentum of

---

1. Letter to William Cathels, in John Barnes, editor, *Portable Australian Author: Joseph Furphy* (St Lucia: University of Queensland Press, 1981), 419.
2. Furphy's Review of *Such Is Life*, in Barnes, 406.
3. Furphy's Review of *Such Is Life*, in Barnes, 3. Hereafter all page references given in my text.

Original Impress has been tending towards this far-off, divine event ever since a scrap of fire-mist flew from the solar centre to form our planet' (1).

Equally seditious to people who support the present Government line, is the fact that its characters are mostly people 'of no fixed address', bullock drivers (who in the days before the coming of the railways provided transport for settlers in the outback, carting supplies to them and bringing their wool back on the return trip) and drovers, people who existed on the fringes of society and had scant respect for Establishment manners, values and pieties. They would not, I suspect, have been impressed by the invocation of 'Australian values' for political purposes, being far too busy learning to deal with the realities confronting ordinary people on the frontier. One of them, the bullock driver, 'Mosey' Price, for instance, mocks the myth of Burke and Wills, dismissing Wills as a 'pore harmless weed' but attacking Burke for his aristocratic pretensions—'Don't sicken a man with yer Burke. He burked that expegition, right enough."Howlt! *Dis*-MOUNT!" Grand style o' man for such a contract! I tell you, that (explorer) died for want of sherry an' biscakes.'—and for his incompetent bushcraft, declaring that 'there ain't a drover, nor yet a bullock driver, nor yet a stock-keeper, from 'ere to 'ell that couldn't a bossed that expegition straight through to the Gulf, an' back agen, an' never turned a hair—with such a season as Burke had' (26).

Burke relied on his image as a 'gentleman'. But for Alf images counted for nothing. What mattered was to confront a difficult environment relying on courage, commonsense and with the help of others, simply doing their job. His attack on the myth is based on his respect for these people and their achievements and he spoke with the authority of experience, having travelled through that country himself and knowing that his father had passed by Burke's camp and been scandalised by all the 'paravinalia' he had which even included a cupboard designed to fit on one of the camels 'for his swell toggery, an' . . . one o' the compartments made to hold his bell-topper' (27). Evidently his attitude to the present culture which according to Jean Baudrillard 'rests on the exaltation of signs based on the denial of the reality of things'[4] would be profoundly subversive and he would have agreed with the epigraph to *Tristram Shandy*, a book similarly

---

4.   Jean Baudrillard, *Revenge Of The Crystal* (Sydney: Pluto Press, 1990), 63.

fascinated with the uses of social signals (a book which Furphy also admired) that 'it is not things that upset men but their judgements about things.'

Not surprisingly then Furphy had little time for empire in general and for the British Empire in particular, believing that they had no respect for the individual but were 'committed to . . . usages of petrified injustice . . . clogged by . . . fealty to shadowy idols, enshrined by Ignorance, and upheld by misplaced homage alone' (66). His hope, however, was that Australia might become a different kind of society whose temper, as he said of his book, would be 'democratic' and its bias 'offensively Australian'. So it is not difficult to imagine what he would think of the Prime Minister who celebrated the centenary of the Australian nation with a visit to London and glories in his friendship with the US President.

Nevertheless Furphy's nationalism is relatively subtle, not so much, as someone has said, a matter of 'what a gum tree looks like but what a gum tree means'. What it meant for him had to do with the interplay between self and the environment as well as self and others. So he had no desire to recreate 'a new Britannia in another world' as many of the more privileged settlers wanted to do. He acknowledged the sheer difference of the place from anything on the other side of the world. As he saw it the environment was one which cut human pretentiousness down to size: 'We are all walking along the shelving edge of a precipice; any one of us may go at any moment, or be dragged down by another' (94). There is nothing here of our current overweening confidence in technology and the Global Economy. The book's opening scene sets the tone, reminding me of Pascal's description of the infinity of space and our finitude, showing Tom making his way across the Riverina plain under the 'geodesic curve' of the sky as 'the dark boundary of the scrub country disappears northward in the glassy haze, and, in front, southward, the level black plains of Riverina Proper mark a straight sky-line'[5] (4).

It is true that one could link this with 'the vision splendid / Of the sunlit plains extended' which underpins the colonial myth of 'development'. But, as Paul Carter points out, that is a myth in which 'Nature's painted curtains are drawn aside to reveal heroic man at his

---

5.　Paul Carter, *The Road To Botany Bay* (London: Faber & Faber, 1987), xv.

heroic labour on the stage of history'[6] (5). But Furphy's view of our place in the scheme of things is anything but heroic. He attacks the Burke and Wills expedition, for example, because heroic pretension prevailed over understanding of the land and respect for its power. The attempted Wills expedition, for instance, comes from his contempt for its failure to take land's power into account and attempting, instead, to impose their ways on it. In contrast, with bullockies like Mosey Alf who had learned to respect it, knowing that if they did not the country itself would '(adj) pretty quickly fetch [them] to [their] proper (adj) level' (26).

There are many examples of this: the swagman who dies of thirst, exhaustion and 'the final collapse of hope' (80) in sight of Rory O'Halloran's hut, of Rory's daughter who wanders away from home, loses her way and dies in the bush, of settlers driven off the land by droughts and floods as well by the 'dirty tricks' of people richer and more powerful than they. As O'Halloran puts it, looking down on the dead body of the swagman and reflecting on he land's 'levelling power: "We're poor helpless craythurs Tammas."' (80). All of this, of course, questions the arrogance of devotees of 'development' today and their remarkable indifference to danger signs in the world around us.

Essentially, then, Furphy was sceptical of power unless it took account of this kind of physical reality and preferred the needs of the powerless to the powerful. As a representative figure Tom is therefore a self-ironic figure, describing himself as having been a government official, of the ninth class; paid rather according to my grade than my merit, and not in proportion to the loafing I had to do' (4). His experience of the outback is the main source of this scepticism. Position and wealth count for little here where droughts, floods and fires on the one hand, and booms and bust in the economy, meant that there existed even fewer rich men who could not imagine a combination of circumstances that would have given [them] lodgings under the bridge?—that may still do so, say, within twelve months?' (94).

The figure of Willoughby, an English gentleman down on his luck, exemplifies this precariousness. His education and sense of social superiority have made rendered him unable to adapt to a situation in which 'urbane address, faultless syntax . . . [and] the

---

6. This comes from a passage in *Such Is Life* which was edited out but published separately as *Rigby's Romance*.

calm consciousness of inherent superiority, are of little use.' Tom sees him as a 'poor shadow of departed exclusiveness as he sits among the bullock drivers around the campfire dependent on their help and hospitality and reflects that 'without doubt it is easier to acquire gentlemanly deportment than axe-man's muscle' (32) but that in the situation in which they find themselves the latter is essential and the former largely irrelevant.

Obviously, this interrogates a culture in which, as Marshall McLuhan put it, it is necessary to 'love one's label as oneself'. But it could be argued that even, or perhaps especially in it, the meaning of human worth which preoccupied Furphy and others like him may still demand consideration. For one thing today, physical reality is beginning to reassert its claims in the environmental crisis confronting us. For another it could be argued that rule by rhetoric, by words with little foundation in fact, undermines the social fabric since as a form of dishonesty it damages trust and understanding. Furphy understood this, as one occasion in which Tom uses this tactic suggests—admittedly in a good cause, trying to persuade the unsympathetic boundary rider Sollicker to return to a sick bullocky the bullocks he confiscated from him while he was lying incapacitated in his camp.

Visiting Sollicker at home and noticing his small son Tom tries to flatter him, invoking the idea then fashionable of the 'Coming Australian', and tells him that the boy is one of 'a race of people . . . such as the world has never seen before' (143). But the strategy fails and Tom reflects that 'nothing is easier than to build Nankin palaces of porcelain theory, which will fall in splinters before the first canon shot of unparleying fact' and that he had no authority to 'dogmatise about the 'Coming Australian'—a version in his day of our talk about 'Australian values'—and that in fact this kind of talk 'is a problem' and concluding that 'deductive reasoning of this [sloganizing] kind is seldom safe' (144).

The 'unparleying fact' he relied on was of the physical, social and economic reality which confronted the people he described attempting to make their way in a difficult environment. He was contemptuous of those who would romanticise the situation. He particularly despised 'novels of the *Geoffrey Hamlyn* class . . . [like] Henry Kingsley's exceedingly trashy and misleading novel' which was peopled, he thought, with 'slender-witted, virgin-souled, overgrown schoolboys' (164), totally unfitted to life on the frontier, contrasting them with writers like Zola: 'He is honest; he never calls evil, good' (245). So one can imagine what Furphy would have to say about contemporary advertising, the masters of spin who guide our rulers and manage much of our media.

For him the foundation of life in society was ethical, the well-being of every person, regardless of social position and wealth. So he was profoundly critical of the society around him which failed to ensure this for the powerless men and women who people his book for whom mere survival often involved a series of 'dirty transactions' (12). One of the bullockies makes this point in an early scene which describes them preparing to let their bullocks on to station land to graze for the night. This was illegal since it involved 'stealing' the grass which' belonged' to the station owner. So Tom, the former bureaucrat remarks that 'this would appear a dirty transaction'. To which one of them, Thompson, replies: "'If you want a problem to work out, just consider that God constructed cattle for living on grass, and the grass to live on, and that, last night, and tonight, and tomorrow night, and mostly every night, we've a choice between two dirty transactions— one is, to let the bullocks starve, and the other is to steal grass for them.'" (12).

Furphy's comment on this dilemma is to conclude the scene by returning to the cosmic perspective with which *Such Is Life* begins, signalling a tension between the law of society and a more universal sense of right and wrong—a tension which still exists today, especially in matters of public policy, even if it is seldom referred to. So Thompson describes the injustice of his situation: "'I'm sick and tired of studying why some people should be in a position where they have to go out of their way to do wrong, and other people are cornered to the extent that they can't live without doing wrong'" (12). But then the narrative pits beyond this situation, seditiously drawing attention to the much larger order of reality:

> It was a clear but moonless night; the dark blue canopy spangled with myriad stars—grandeur, peace and purity above; squalor, worry, and profanity below. Fit basis for many an ancient system of Theology—unscientific, if you will, but by no means contemptible (13).

It is by opening up this perspective, I suggest, that Furphy is most subversive since it points to the need to redefine current one-dimensional notions of reality and value. In this long perspective money and social position are of little account. So it is possible for one of his characters to declare: "'We draw no colour line, no educational line, not even an intellectual line, but we fix a very distinct standard of progress potential'" (333).[7]—which in this context would mean the obligation to ensure that each person is able to achieve dignity and satisfaction. Tom points to this obligation on another occasion, for example, when he remarks: 'Heaven knows I am no more inclined to decry social culture than moral principle; but I acknowledge no aristocracy except one of service and self-sacrifice in which he that is chief shall be servant of all, and he that is greatest of all, servant of all' (33).

This sense of obligation to the other is not fashionable today, and it certainly subverts the way competition tends to prevail over cooperation, installing the supremacy of might over right. So Furphy suspects the value placed on 'success', usually defined in economic terms, being aware of its human cost, and thus interrogates the narrative of 'progress', describing the 'successful pioneer', for example, as 'the early bird' and the 'forgotten pioneer' as 'the early worm.' The former 'is the man who never spared others; [the latter] the man who never spared himself, but, being a fool, built houses for wise men to live in, and omitted to gather moss', making a Raleigh-cloak of himself to afford free and 'pleasant passage for the noblest work of God, namely, the Business Man' (86). This could surely be seen by many today as blasphemy indeed.

But this, to refer belatedly to it, is the reason for the disjunctive nature of his narrative which reflects his ironic sense of reality and of our ambiguous place in it which contrasts markedly with the self-confident belief that human beings are in charge of the universe which, despite all the evidence to the contrary, underpins our culture. As one critic points out *a propos* Pascal's fragmentary way of setting out his philosophy, disjuncture may be the best way to break out of a monolithic world view into a larger sense of reality:

---

7.   William Goldmann, *Le Dieu Cache* (Paris: Gallimard, 1955), 37.

> Pascal's message is that Man is great in that he searches for absolute values but small in that, without ever ceasing to search, he knows that he can never approach these values. The only form to express this context is . . . one which does not prove the contrary; which does not show either [someone] who has abandoned the search or one who has approached the goal. The fragment is such a form (7).

Furphy, too, a post-modernist before his time, rejects grand narratives to focus on the task of living in a complex and challenging universe, refusing to accept an identity imposed from outside by society, affirming his own responsibility and the risky ambiguities of his situation. But this, paradoxically, is what makes his world view so cheerfully creative—in contrast with the anxieties underneath the surface of the apparent self-confidence of Western culture today. It is creative because, as a life which is properly human involves a going beyond the facts, an acceptance of generous fancies, a projection of our sentiments and inner activities on the forms we perceive about us (and a recognition from this interaction of ourselves, our inner world) . . . We are all of us, insofar as we interact morally and politically, fanciful projectors, makers and believers in fictions and metaphors.[8]

Martha Nussbaum argues:

> Put another way, the sense of vast unconsciousness of nature which pervades Furphy's work leads ultimately to the agnostic sense of the vast nature of consciousness with which *Such Is Life* concludes: Such is life, my fellow mummers—just like a poor player, that bluffs and feints his hour upon the stage, and then cheapens down to mere nonentity. But let me not hear any small witticism to the further effect that its story is a tale told by a vulgarian, full of slang and blanky, signifying—nothing (297).

If this is subversive, this kind of subversion may be badly needed today.

---

8. Martha Nussbaum, *Poetic Justice: The Literary Imagination And Political Life* (Boston: 1995), 24.

An Incident In The Culture Wars:
Judith Wright's 'Haunted Land'

We begin with a passage from Judith Wright's family history *The Generations Of Men* in which she imagines her grandfather, one of the early settlers on the New England tableland, reflecting on the fate of the Aboriginal people who had had been a flourishing and dignified community when he and his family had arrived but were now reduced to a diseased and bedraggled minority. Surprisingly, however, Wright has him suspect that he and his fellow newcomers had also been damaged in the encounter, imagining their 'whole civilisation haunted, like a house haunted by the ghost of a dead man buried under it' but also 'by [a] deep and festering consciousness of guilt in themselves.'[1] This is evidently a 'Black Armband' approach to history. But before considering the issues this raises, we need to define what is meant by the word 'Australia' and to what extent it can be seen as a 'thinking society and culture'.

I begin by seeing the two as more or less synonymous, if a nation is defined as an 'imagined community', that is as an ideological construct. I then go on to suggest that there may be serious flaws in the way in which we have imagined ourselves, pointing to the limitations of cultural premises underlying it which are those of the Enlightenment and the attempts to impose European hegemony which grew out of it. I find an essay by a Brazilian sociologist Luiz Carlos Susin illuminating here. He argues that the identity thus generated rests on the story of Ulysses who left home and travelled through strange places intended to return home again or to conquering these places and make them like home. In effect then this story describes 'a closed

---

1. Judith Wright, *The Generations Of Men* (Melbourne: Oxford University Press, 1965), 163.

circle around sameness'[2] from within which the self sallies forth to conquer difference, 'distinguishing and identifying good and evil in a very particular way, based on itself, on its glorious position as basis and referent of the whole of reality spread out at its feet.[3]

I think this is a reasonably accurate description of Australia today. But it goes back to the beginnings of settlement, to settlers like WC Wentworth, for instance, who declared his intention to build 'A new Britannia in another world'.[4] The architecture of nineteenth century cities, Melbourne especially, witness to a similar attempt. But it set up a disjunction between the self and its actual environment and signal a determination to destroy its difference and to remake it to the image of our desires. So, drawing on accounts of the arrival of the First Fleet, Paul Carter argues that the place figured in them 'simply [as] a stage where history occurred' and that this history was in effect 'a theatrical performance . . . a fabric of self-reinforcing illusions' and the land was a kind of stage on which 'Nature's painted curtains [were] drawn aside to reveal heroic man at his epic labour on the stage of history'.[5]

This refusal to deal with difference is central to Patrick White's *Voss,* his meditation on the myth of the explorer in the contrast it draws between the Bonners and their circle who cling to the fringes of the self, shrinking from 'the deep end of the unconscious'[6] as they shrink from the interior of the continent and Voss and his party who respond to the challenge of the interior. I would also suggest that it is evident today and that a society deeply suspicious of difference is not likely to be a thinking society or culture. In the twenty-first century ahead it may be even more out of touch with reality and problematic than it is today. But it is not the only model of identity.

Susin offers an alternative, a model which is open rather than closed, based on the figure of Abraham who left his familiar world and culture in response to a 'call to go further' to move across the known horizon. But it should also be noted that this model implies a return to an ontology and epistemology which gives credence to realities beyond those which are rational, material and measurable. It also supports Mircea Eliade's proposition that the primary task of

---

2.   Luiz Carlos Susin, 'A Critique Of The Identity Paradigm', in *Concilium*, 2 (2000): 87.

3.   Susin, 'A Critique Of The Identity Paradigm', 80.

4.   Ian Turner, editor, *The Australian Dream* (Melbourne: Sun Books, 1968), 12.

5.   Paul Carter, *The Road To Botany Bay* (London: Faber & Faber, 1988), xiv–xv.

6.   Patrick White, *Flaws In The Glass* (London: Cape, 1981), 104.

a people newly arrived in a country hitherto unknown to them is metaphysical rather than merely economic, the 'transformation of chaos into cosmos',[7] to find their place there in some larger scheme of things.

A strain running through our literary and artistic culture has pursued this task from the beginning, often against the grain of the larger culture which has been largely dominated by neo-Darwinian and neo-Utilitarian modes of thinking and feeling. Where this culture was largely intent on dominating the land and making it serve our purposes and ignoring the wisdom of its First Peoples, this strain tended to see the land more as a metaphysical than as an economic resource. In *Such Is Life,* for instance, Joseph Furphy's Tom Collins declares that 'the Australian attains full consciousness of his own nationality' in the interior, seeing the land itself which he sees as anything but subservient to our intentions but as 'grave, subdued, self-centred', an other which demands respect but which also contain 'a latent meaning' to be 'faithfully and lovingly interpreted'.[8] Many subsequent writers, artists and musicians have made similar suggestions, though there is no time to explore their work here.

Instead let us return to Judith Wright since she brings together a number of factors necessary for the formation of a thinking culture and society by connecting literary concerns with political, historical, sociological and even economic issues. While it is true therefore that the passage we have been discussing could be said to belong to a 'Black Armband' school of history it also enables us to situate the 'History Wars' in a more wide-ranging and therefore more intellectually respectable context, seeing it as a clash between two different world views and thus of ideas of national identity.

As she describes her grandfather he is in fact torn between them. He is aware on the one hand that he is one of the conquerors who displaced the land's Aboriginal owners and were destroying their culture. But on the other he has a feeling, a 'queer sympathy' with one of them the old black fellow Paddy, one of his workers, and the culture which enabled him to 'answer his moods with an understanding [he] seldom found among white men, who, intent on their own interests

---

7. Mircea Eliade, *The Myth Of The Eternal Return* (Princeton: Princeton University Press, 1974), 10.
8. John Barnes, editor, *Portable Australian Authors: Joseph Furphy* (St Lucia: Queensland University Press, 1981), 65.

and problems, took little notice of the needs of other people'.[9] Unlike many of his contemporaries, however, Albert Wright is troubled by this sensitivity and does not see it as a sign of inferiority. Rather it makes him question his own culture which in its pursuit of 'money, security, prosperity', in 'a whirlwind of destruction', seems to him to be 'speaking words of power, but not words of life'.[10]

Here Wright is interrogating the founding story of our identity which is 'the permanent secret of [our]meaning and obligation'.[11] To the extent that in it the self alone is the arbiter of good and evil and acknowledges no authority beyond it, it could be seen as ethically deficient. That is at least if one accepts Emmanuel Levinas' proposition that it is only 'in the laying down by the ego of its sovereignty . . . that we find ethics and also perhaps the very spirituality of the soul, but most certainly the question of the meaning of being, that is, its appeal for justification.'[12] Moreover, in this view justification does not depend upon some abstract and anonymous law, or judicial entity, 'but by the extent to which one is aware of an act upon one's responsibility for the other'[13] for other human beings, but also by the natural world on which we depend.

This takes us back to the Abrahamic model of identity which is open and responsive to the other and to move out of the 'closed circle around sameness' towards it. In refusing to do this, as Wright argues, we have suffered a 'mortal wound . . . a deep and festering consciousness of guilt'. In turn, the anxiety and pain caused has fuelled the 'hatred and contempt that so many . . . held for the blacks' which is often used to justify our treatment of them. Until it is dealt with, she believed, it 'would remain forever at the root of this country, making every achievement empty and every struggle vain'.[14]

This is not the kind of argument most of us are accustomed to conduct. But it is not to say that it may not be worth doing so. Reflecting over the debates which followed the High Court's Mabo judgement, Raimond Gaita makes this point: 'One should not, as critics of Mabo tend to do, to restrict the concept of national interest

---

9. Wright, *The Generations Of Men,* 159.
10. Wright, *The Generations Of Men,* 161.
11. Susin, 'A Critique Of The Identity Paradigm', 81.
12. Sean Hand, editor, *The Levinas Reader* (Oxford: Blackwell, 1993), 85.
13. Hand, *The Levinas Reader,* 82.
14. Wright, *The Generations Of Men,* 163.

to economic interests or to the interest of having an undivided body politic . . . Even in politics, we are, inescapably, moral beings.'[15] We are all ultimately responsible moral beings responsible to one another since, as John Donne famously put it, no one is an island but each of us is part of the one great continent of life.

Once more it is worth returning to the original experience of settlement in which, to put it simply, perhaps over-simply, we attempted to impose time, the linear time of imperial history on place and the might of this, our endowment as evolution's spearhead, was right. The fact that the land and its First Peoples resisted only intensified our determination to assert our assert, our domination over these First Peoples and the land. Far from laying down or even diminishing its authority by acknowledging the claims of what is other-than-self (which Levinas sees as the properly ethical position) the ego asserted it. As Ian Turner sees it:

> These new Australians were involved with moulding an untouched and often intransigent environment to their will. A religion which was appropriate for the ordered society and regular living of rural England seemed irrelevant to pioneering labour in the Australian bush. Men carved their own lives out of a remote and monstrously difficult wilderness; what they achieved, they owed to themselves, and they found little for which to thank their fathers' heaven.[16]

To draw on the taxonymy developed by Helene Cixous,[17] this is an essentially 'masculine' position, within the 'economy of the proper', which is concerned with property, propriety and appropriation. It thus circles around itself and is suspicious of the other, assuming that 'the moment you receive something you are effectively "open" to the other, and . . . you have only one wish . . . hastily to return the gift, to break the circuit of an exchange that could have no end . . . to be nobody's child, to owe no one a thing.'[18] In contrast the 'feminine', the 'economy of the gift', echoes the story of Abraham since it gives to

---

15. Raimond Gaita, 'Guilt, Shame and Collective Responsibility', in Michelle Grattan, editor *Essays On Australian Reconciliation* (Melbourne: Black Inc, 2000), 278.

16. Turner, *The Australian Dream*, x.

17. Toril Moi, *Sexual/ Textual Politics: Feminist Literary Theory* (London: Routledge, 1991), 110–113.

18. Moi, *Sexual/ Textual Politics: Feminist Literary Theory*, 112.

and receives from the other, moving across boundaries and open to new understandings and attentive to the 'resonance of fore-language . . . the language of 1,000 tongues which knows neither enclosure nor death.'[19]

This is the way Wright and indeed many others like her lived. As a child she spent a good deal of time alone exploring the family property. As she put it later: 'Most children are . . . are brought up in the 'I' tradition these days—the ego, it's me and what I think. But when you live in very close contact with a large and splendid landscape you feel yourself a good deal smaller than just I.'[20] For her the land was not just an empty space to be filled with crops and animals but a living presence in which she sensed a story which interrogated that of her own people and history.

'Bora Ring', one of her early poems, is a good example not only of her sense of this presence but also of the claims it makes, opening with a sense that their

> . . . song is gone; the dance
> is secret with the dancers in the earth,
> the ritual useless, and the tribal story
> lost in an alien tale—

but concluding with an acceptance of responsibility for this loss as

> . . . the rider's heart
> halts at a sightless shadow, and unsaid word
> that fastens in the blood the ancient curse,
> the fear as old as Cain.[21]

This brings us to the crux of the argument over 'Black Armband' history, the charge that it is the product of bleeding hearts rather than intelligent minds.

But I would contend that this kind of acceptance of responsibility for past events is more hard-headed than the guilt which actually underlies this charge, at least if we accept Paul Ricoeur's definition

---

19. Moi, *Sexual/ Textual Politics: Feminist Literary Theory*, 113.
20. Veronica Brady, *South Of My Days: A Biography Of Judith Wright* (Sydney: Angus & Robertson, 1998), 469.
21. Judith Wright, *Collected Poems 1942–1985* (Sydney: Angus & Robertson, 1994), 8.

of guilt as 'feeling responsible for not being responsible'.[22] This is a definition which suggests its links with the anxieties and over-reaction evident in our dealings with Aboriginal Australia. Martin Buber, suggests a way of dealing with this problem writing that 'the idea of responsibility needs to be brought back from the province of a specialised ethics; of an "ought" that swings free in the air, into that of real life'.[23]

Wright does this in one of her later poems, 'the Dark Ones'[24], set in a typical country town on pension day, the day when Aboriginal fringe-dwellers, otherwise invisible come to town to collect their government hand-outs. The poem's focus is on the whites' reaction to their appearance, first of all on their anxiety and then on its source, implying that for them the Aborigines represent the shadow side of the self, its negative aspect, 'the sum of all the unpleasant qualities we like to hide, together with the insufficiently developed functions and the contents of the personal unconscious'.[25]

> On the other side of the road
> the dark ones stand.
> Something leaks in our blood
> like the ooze from a wound.

Then it goes on to suggest the way in which their continuing existence challenges the sense of self which depends on the imperial story in which they figure as the spearhead of the evolution which, at the other end of its scale, has doomed them to give way before us and die out:

> A shudder like breath caught
> runs through the town.
> Are *they* still here? We thought . . .
> Let us alone.

This identity, as we have been arguing, takes no responsibility for anyone or anything other than the self and its interests. Against this Raimond Gaita quotes Martin Buber: 'The idea of responsibility needs to be brought back from the province of a specialised ethics;

---

22. Paul Ricoeur, *The Symbolism Of Evil* (Boston: Beacon Press. 1969), 21.
23. Wright, *Collected Poems*, 354–355.
24. Gaita, 'Guilt, Shame and Collective Responsibility', in Grattan, 284.
25. Anthony Storr, *Jung: Selected Writings* (London, Fontana Press, 1983), 87.

of an "ought" that swings free in the air, into that that of real life. Genuine responsibility exists only when there is real responding.'[26] The definition of 'real life' is implicit in Gaita's further point that the story by which we make sense of our lives should exist 'against the background of compassionate responsiveness to the defining vulnerability of a common human condition.'[27] So I conclude that a thinking society and thinking culture, which will enable to negotiate the challenging future ahead of us needs to take this into account.

26. Gaita, 'Guilt, Shame and Collective Responsibility', in Grattan, 284.
27. Gaita, 'Guilt, Shame and Collective Responsibility', in Grattan, 284.

After Cronulla:
The Defence Of The 'White Earth'

Violence, culture and identity are closely bound in a settler society like Australia.

According to Deborah Bird Rose, the space we inhabit is 'wounded' and most of us are marked by the 'epistemic violence' (Gayatri Spivak) of colonisation, and this, I suggest, was evident at Cronulla recently. But assertions of this kind are difficult to explore, belonging as they do to the unconscious, the dimension of 'the archaic, the nocturnal, the oneiric'.[1] But symbols, 'the surveyor's staff and guide for "becoming oneself"'[2] and also the stuff of fiction may provide access. So let me base my argument on an exploration of Andrew McGahan's 1995 Miles Franklin award winning novel, *The White Earth*.[3]

According to the author it expresses a premonition that Australia is 'on the verge of something very dark and ugly politically'[4]—which perhaps surfaced at Cronulla. The novel's tone is Gothic, full of images of decay and excess centred on a decaying mansion, a kind of fortress in which its aging megalomaniac owner John McIvor attempts to 'hold his beliefs against the world'[5]—image, if you like, the Fortress Australia mentality of the present government. But where the lines between good and evil are usually clearly drawn in melodrama it is ambiguous here since the story is filtered through the confusedly

---

1. Paul Ricoeur, *The Symbolism Of Evil* (Boston: Beacon Press, 1969), 34.
2. Ricoeur, *The Symbolism Of Evil*, 13.
3. Andrew Mc Gahan, *The White Earth*. Sydney (Melbourne: Allen & Unwin, 2004). All page references will be given hereafter in my text.
4. James Ley, 'How Small The Lights Of Home: Andrew Mc Gahan And The Politics Of Guilt', in *Australian Book Review,* 280 (April 2006): 35 I am very much indebted to this paper essay in my paper.
5. Ley, 'How Small The Lights Of Home', 38.

impressionable eyes of McIvor's nephew William—suggesting a more general crisis of value within the culture as a whole. William's ineffectual father has died in an accident and his mother is a figure of angry weakness so that the boy is dependent on the rich uncle who wants to indoctrinate him with his values. As James Ley notes therefore, William is a figure of *anomie* who finds himself in a situation he can neither understand nor control and lacks the ability and will to remove himself, allowing himself to be carried uneasily along by event[6]—and perhaps there is a parallel between him and many of the participants in the events at Cronulla, so unsure of themselves that their identity seemed to depend on killing a common enemy.[7]

The novel as a whole reaches its climax moment in a similar confrontation, a rally against Aboriginal land rights legislation which Mc Ivor organises on his property. He is a much stronger character, a figure of *ressentiment,* an embodiment of white fantasies of privilege and power which, paradoxically, arise from and often return to the feelings of disintegration and insignificance which arise from being unsure of one's place in the scheme of things.[8] His father was the manager of Kuran station which had belonged for generations to a rich pioneering family, heirs of privilege which he envied and aspired to. His son becomes a means to this end as he brings him up to believe that his destiny is to marry the only child of the house, a daughter. But class is an insuperable barrier and John is reminded of his social insignificance when she refuses to have anything to do with him. Humiliated, he decides to make Kuran by his own one day by sheer force of determination, sacrificing everything else and alienating his wife and daughter in the process. To ensure that he keeps control even after his death he brings John and his mother to Kuran to guarantee the succession.

In this way McIvor is a 'self-made man', the type of a new society. In traditional societies identity depends on finding one's place in it. But he makes it by an effort of will, exerting himself against his circumstances as he pursues his goal of property and power, suspicious of and hostile to anyone or anything which threatens to

---

6. Ley, 'How Small The Lights Of Home', 35.
7. Rene Girard, 'The God Of Victims', in Graham Ward, editor, *The Postmodern God: A Theological Reader* (Oxford: Wiley-Blackwell, 1998), 105–115.
8. Ghassan Hage, *White Nation: Fantasies Of White Supremacy In A Multi-Cultural Society* (Sydney: Pluto Press, 1998).

impede him—hence his opposition to Aboriginal land claims. The Charter of the movement he founds to contest Aboriginal land rights which, incidentally, resembles the aims of Pauline Hanson's One Nation, reflects this ferocious and paranoid individualism and a patriotism which is largely a projection of his anxieties—which also may also be true of the flag-waving rioters at Cronulla.

Those who deny the shadow side of the self imagine they actually are only what they care to know about themselves. So McIvor's patriotism rests on the conviction that his own culture and values are right and superior to all others, 'lesser breeds without the law'. Untroubled by self-reflection he is a law unto himself (128) like the early settlers he admires for whom in effect might equalled right, believing in what he calls 'the inherent value of Australian culture and traditions' which he believes guarantee that 'the rights of the individual cannot be interfered with' (133). Accordingly, William, his uncle's obedient echo, responds to the challenge of Aboriginal land claims by asserting that 'Australia is our place now! You can't make us give it back!' (284)—assuming, incidentally, that Aborigines are not 'Australian'.

In effect they belong to a culture which has ignored what Mircea Eliade sees as the primary task for any people settling into a country hitherto unknown to them, the 'transformation of chaos into cosmos',[9] a task which is essentially imaginative rather than material. Ironically Mc Ivor's is obsessed with the land. He tells William, for instance:

> You have to know about a piece of land . . . if you're going to own it. You have to know where it fits in . . . Every stretch of land has its own story. You have to listen, and understand how it connects with other stories. Stories that involve the whole country in the end (106).

But this is because he regards it as his own possession and a resource to be exploited. Locked in his 'closed circle around sameness'[10] and sharing its allergy to the indefinite and impossible to explain, he refuses to yield to any power other than his own. He may say that

---

9. Mircea Eliade, *The Myth Of The Eternal Return Or, Cosmos And History* (Princeton, Princeton University Press, 1974), 10.

10. Luiz Carlos Susin, 'A Critique Of The Identity Paradigm', in *Cross Currents*, 2 (2002): 87.

'[t]his place is alive in its own right'. But he sees that life in his own ideological terms, 'growing and changing all the time' (85), subjecting it to the logic of 'progress' and 'development', the logic of imperial history which, he believes, gives him his 'glorious position as basis and referent of the whole of reality spread out at [his] feet'.[11] As it drives towards the future it leaves the past behind. 'The Aborigines are gone . . . This is my property now' (209). They are 'not coming back.' (100)

The novel contradicts this, however. The land has a life of its own which finally brings Mc Ivor undone. He dies in the fire which destroys the house which he thinks he has made his own, consumed by the reality he has denied. So too, the rally against Aboriginal land rights which he organises with an explosion of fiery violence as the 'ethical terror'[12] which in fact underlies the rally reaches its climax. Once again fire, symbol of the sacred and of the land's power, prevails. Nor has the past been obliterated. The Aborigines have not 'died out' and the land continues to remember them. When, exploring the property, William comes upon the deep pool, once a ceremonial place, he smells 'blood and death' (300). The survivors of the Aboriginal people who had been displaced by the whites had kept coming back there. But finally, the whites, determined to assert their possession, killed them and burned the bodies which they then threw into the pool to conceal what they had done. For Mc Ivor, however, it was an important place because it was a permanent source of water. But the boy senses 'something invisible [there which] had made the air too potent to Breathe . . . some cold and ancient secret of the land itself' (326).

Mc Gahan seems to be echoing here Judith Wright's intuition that Australian culture. can be compared to a house which is haunted by the 'ghost of a murdered man buried under it'. The novel's conclusion also echoes her suggestion that until it is confronted this anxiety 'would remain forever at the root of this country, making every achievement empty and every struggle vain'.[13] William is important here. Until now, seduced by the prospect of inheriting Kuran and fascinated by his ferocious certainties he has been his uncle's echo and

---

11. Susin, 'A Critique Of The Identity Paradigm', 80.
12. Ricoeur, *The Symbolism Of Evil*, 29.
13. Judith Wright, *The Generations Of Men* (Melbourne: Oxford University Press, 19650), 163.

enthralled by what holds him captive, an example of what Ricoeur calls 'the servile will'.[14] But he has caught occasional glimpses of a past whose 'truth was thirst and heat and twisted ghosts' and begins to realise that inheriting Kuran would be 'no gift . . . [but] a burden' (327). Here the Aboriginal story speaks to him and later even more strongly when McIvor's disaffected daughter, a lawyer and advocate of Aboriginal land rights puts their case.

In effect he is moving out of his culture's 'closed circle around sameness'. According to Emmanuel Levinas this marks the beginning of a genuinely ethical existence. 'It is in the laying down by the ego of its sovereignty (in its hateful modality) [he writes] that we find ethics and also probably the very spirituality of the soul, but most certainly the question of the meaning of being.'[15] It is significant therefore that as the novel ends William is recovering from an operation to cure him of the ear infection he has been suffering which, also significantly, was caused by violence, by a blow from his angrily unhappy mother.

I conclude then that the connection between violence, identity and mainstream Australian culture is largely the product of the 'hateful modality of the self' which has developed within it but that this connection can be broken by a return to what Levinas calls a 'non-intentional consciousness' which recognises the claims of what is other-than-self, preferring 'that which justified being over that which assures it.

---

14. Ricoeur, *The Symbolism Of Evil*, 100.
15. Sean Hand, editor, *The Levinas Reader* (Oxford: Wiley-Blackwell, 1993), 85.

An Apology For The Library And For 'The Golden World Of The Imagination': A Neo-Luddite View

I begin by recalling where we are, in the first place on land cared for and celebrated by its Aboriginal inhabitants since time immemorial and secondly on monastery land which is also hallowed, and I do this as a neo-Luddite. The original Luddites, as you know, opposed the introduction of industrial machinery, wanting to preserve the craft tradition. But as Karl Marx pointed out, something was also lost with the introduction of mass-production. In a way the hand-craftsman or–woman at could be said to make him/herself in the process of working, the factory worker merely makes money. Similarly in *Utopia* St Thomas More, discussing the enclosures of his day as large landowners were evicting peasants to turn agricultural land into pasture for sheep—much more profitable—noted that this was a reversal of the proper order of things: once men used to eat sheep, he said, but now 'the sheep eateth up the men'.

I call myself a Luddite, though a 'neo' one, for similar reasons since I also believe in the importance of tradition (which someone has defined as 'running errands for the dead', continuing the work they began), and do not believe that everything new is automatically better than everything old or that the primary task of libraries, for instance, is to provide information.

Central to the work of civilisation (according to the Macquarie Dictionary 'the state of society in which a high level of art, science and government has been reached'), I suggest, is the task of preserving and, if possible, expanding that state. For a variety of reasons, this seems to be growing increasingly difficult today. But libraries are an essential resource. To put it in slogan form, they are crucial for the future as well as for the present because they preserve the past. What do I mean by that?

Most of you, I suspect, would agree that the present is not very inspiring. But we need to ask why this is so and what that situation may be asking of us. First of all, I would point to the need to be realistic, not to succumb to he blandishments of a culture 'distracted by distraction from distraction' and to pretend that all is well when clearly in so many respects it is not. One of Gunter Grass' novels, *The Rat*, is about this evasion. It is set in the future after civilisation has been destroyed by a nuclear holocaust. The sole survivor is a rat who looks back on the last days before this end and reflects on the gap which then existed between reality and peoples' refusal to acknowledge it as they clung to their illusions:

> Our intention was that men should learn
> little by little
> to handle not only knife and fork
> but one another as well, and reason too
> that omnipotent can opener.
>
> That once educated, the human race should freely,
> yes, freely, determine its destiny and free from its shackles
> learn to guide nature cautiously,
> as cautiously as possible,
> away from chaos.[1]

A few did, it is true, begin to realise that

> something must be wrong
> I don't know what, the direction maybe.
> Some mistake, but what, has been made
> but when and where wrong,
> especially as everything's been running like clockwork,
> though in a direction
> which signs demonstrate to be wrong (161).

But they refused to accept responsibility and to realise that

> we could all of us, just for the sake of argument, be
> the source of error, yes,
> it could be you or you or you (161).

---

1. Gunter Grass, *The Rat*, translated by Ralph Mannheim (Secker and Warburg 1987), 132. Further page references will be given in my text.

Maybe this is true of us today as problems environmental, social and political accumulate. But to accept this we probably need to look beyond the narrow perspectives of the present and set ourselves in the context of world history on the one hand and on the knowledge with which contemporary science is providing us. We also need, I submit, to embrace notions of right and wrong beyond the self-interest fashionable today, to understand more fully what it means to be properly human and reflect not just on our rights but also on our obligations to ourselves, others and the world to which we belong. By and large, however, we have largely failed to do this and to recognise the crisis confronting us or to realise that, as Grass says, we may be the real source of the problem. Martin Heidegger suggested this half a century ago when he argued that the times we live in are 'destitute' 'not only because God is dead, but [because we] are hardly aware and capable of our own mortality. In effect we have not realised— or perhaps have forgotten the proper nature of our humanity, or we 'have not yet come into ownership of [our] own nature.' As a result 'death withdraws into the enigmatic. The mystery of pain remains veiled. Love has not been learned.'[2]

This is increasingly even clearer today. But, as Samuel Beckett remarked, 'habit is a great deadener'. We have become accustomed to the cruelties and injustices surrounding us and untroubled by them unless they affect us directly. One reason for this, I suggest, is that we have allowed others to imagine the world for us, are gradually losing the ability to get outside our present frame of reference and see ourselves from the perspective of others and of other cultures and periods of history. This means that we have less and less sense of the possibility of other ways of seeing the world and living in it and of the full range of human experience. Trapped in the 'closed circle around sameness' which the media draws around us and intent on what DH Lawrence called the 'business of money-making, money-having and money-spending', we fail to explore the mysteries of 'pain, death and love'.

But libraries enable us to explore them, expanding our understanding of our actual experiences. They also keep us in touch with other cultures and other periods of history and thus with experience different from our own, enabling us, as a friend of mine

2. In Martin Heidegger, *Poetry, Language, Thought* (New York: Colophon Books, 1975), 96.

likes to say, to 'try on other lives for size'. Moreover, they have done this over time—as the fact that we are meeting today at a monastery. It was monastery libraries which kept European civilisation alive, and it has always been one of their tasks to provides time and space for reflection in which to interrogate the reign of matter-of-fact and the direction in which the world may be heading away from the fear and suspicion which makes for the wars and rumours of wars around us. This is a crucial contribution. Kofi Annan, for instance, has warned that lack of sensitivity to other peoples' beliefs could lead to a new war of religion on a global scale. The 'golden world of the imagination', however, can point us elsewhere.

As far as I know Sir Philip Sidney coined this phrase in his *Apology for Poetry*, in which he defended it against the literal-minded of his day, the Puritans, who regarded things imaginative with suspicion, pointing out that most other forms of knowledge have what already exists, 'the works of nature', for principal object and that they could not consist without it and depend on it. But that, he said, makes them 'actors and players, as it were' in preserving things as they are. 'Only the poet [by which he means the person able to create and explore possibilities yet unseen or unrealised], disdaining to be tied to any such subjection, lifted up with the vigour of his own imagination, doth grow in effect another nature, in making things either better than nature bringeth forth, or quite anew.[3]

The poet Wallace Stevens (who, being the well-read man that he was) had probably something similar in mind when he wrote in his 'The Man With The Blue Guitar':

> The man bent over his blue guitar,
> A shearsman of sorts. The day was green.
>
> They said. 'You have a blue guitar,
> You do not play things as they are.'
>
> The man replied, 'Things as they are
> Are changed upon the blue guitar.'
>
> And they said then, 'But play, you must,
> A tune beyond us, yet ourselves,

---

3. In MH Abrams *et al, The Norton Anthology Of English Literature* I. (New York: WW Norton, 1962), 426.

A tune upon the blue guitar
Of things exactly as they are.[4]

The discoveries of Quantum Physics point in the same direction, observing that the observer changes what is observed. Similarly, writers and artists can change our perceptions of the world and thus cause us to act differently. This kind of awareness can bring about the kind of awareness and action which Gunter Grass' novel sees as so urgently necessary today as we are increasingly manipulated by images and ideas imposed on us from the outside and the inner life is neglected in the interests of conformity and fashion.

Martha Nussbaum argues also that this trend has other disturbing implications:

> We should regard with suspicion any claim to rule a nation of human beings by a ruler who does not acknowledge the inner moral life of each human being, its strivings and complexities, its complicated emotions, its efforts at understanding and its terrors, [and which] does not distinguish in its descriptions between a human being and a machine.[5]

Emmanuel Levinas expanded on this when he wrote that 'it is in the laying down by the ego of its sovereignty . . . that we find ethics and also very probably the very spirituality of the soul, but most certainly the question of the meaning of being'[6](6)—something which most of the world's religious traditions have always known.

But 'the meaning of being' is not at the centre of public discussion today, of course. Instead, it seems to be the will of 'the Market' and the state of the economy that tends to be foremost. But the tradition preserved in libraries makes it clear that there are 'more things in heaven and earth than are dreamed of' by *homo economicus*, more expansive, life-giving and creative realities. As Erasmus remarked, 'man is not born man but becomes man'. Every technological advance or historical development therefore calls us to redefine and expand our notions of our humanity.

---

4. Wallace Stevens *Selected Poems* (London: Faber & Faber, 1957), 52.
5. Martha Nussbaum, *Poetic Justice: The literary Imagination And Political Life* (Boston: Beacon Books), 38.
6. Sean Hand, editor, *The Levinas Reader* (Oxford: Blackwell, 1993), 85.

Books which help us to think and feel with, for and through the lives of others obviously have an important part to play in this process. As William Blake pointed out, in an important sense ultimately the world is neither round nor flat but human-shaped: the way things reflect our values and our notions of reality—and the contemporary understanding of the power of ideology confirms this. It is becoming increasingly clear, for example, that a world addicted to the worship what I call the 'Unholy Trinity, Mammon (the god of money), Moloch (the god of violence and competition) and McDonald's (the god of destructive pleasures) threatens our existence as human beings but also the world in which we live and on which we depend.

This throws further light not only on Heidegger's proposition that we live in a 'destitute time' but also on his point that hope remains because 'song (that is, the kind of imaginative thinking and feeling we are talking about) remains': 'the singers still keep to the trace of the holy.'[7] This brings us to the point with which we begin (which we did not consider earlier) that our time is destitute because 'God is dead'—Nietzsche's proposition, of course. Heidegger cancels this out, however, when he argues that the 'singers' refuse to accept this and 'keep to the trace of the holy.' Paul Ricoeur's discussion of the idea that 'God is dead' illuminates what Heidegger is getting at. But it also strengthens the argument for the importance of libraries.

According to Ricoeur 'the true question is to know, first of all, which god is dead; then, who has killed him (if it is true that this death is a murder); and finally, what sort of authority belongs to the announcement of this death.'[8] The god who is dead, he suggests, is an abstraction, the 'First Cause', omnipotent, omniscient and so on and 'out there' who is ultimately perhaps, as Marx argued, merely a human projection of emotional, social, political or economic need, and his death was in effect a suicide since this was no god in the proper sense of the word, a reality beyond human comprehension. So the authority which belongs to the announcement of this death is that of a Living God whose 'being is in coming' who 'goes on ways to himself' 'through this world in our human experience and in the community of belief, even when [these ways] lead to other places,

---

7. Heidegger, *Poetry, Language, Thought*. New York, 97.
8. Paul Ricoeur, *The Conflict Of Interpretations*, edited by Don Idhe (Evanston: Northwestern University Press, 1974), 445.

even to that which is not God',[9] opening up new possibilities for our humanity and for our understanding of the 'privilege and panic' of our mortality and of the mysteries of pain, death and love.

So Martha Nussbaum, to quote her again, can argue:

> A life which is properly human involves a going beyond the facts, an acceptance of generous fancies, a projection of our sentiments and inner activities on the forms we perceive about us (and a recognition from this interaction of images of ourselves, of our own inner world) . . . We are all of us, insofar as we interact morally and politically, fanciful projectors, makers and believers in fictions and metaphors.[10]

Evidently, this brings us back again to the library, where as Milton described it:

> there be pens and heads . . . . sitting by their studious lamps, musing, searching, revolving new notions and ideas wherewith to present, as with their homage and fealty, the approaching Reformation: others as fast reading, trying all things, asserting to the force of reason and convincement. For him the library was a place of creativity in which people could pursue the light which . . . was given to us, not to be ever staring on, but by it to discover onward things more remote from our knowledge.[11]

It is true, of course, that it can be dangerous to organise our lives entirely from books. Ideologues like Hitler and Stalin, not to mention the neo-Cons of our day and Grand Inquisitors of all kinds in the past and present, have done so with destructive consequences for human dignity and integrity. But, as Milton suggests, books which provoke new kinds of understanding as well as information can open up creative gaps and fissures in our present certainties, raise doubts and questions about them and keep alive the hope, 'the long-distance runner', as Gunter Grass calls it, of new and richer possibilities, for us to continue the search for 'the meaning behind the meaning' of

9. Eberhard Jüngel, *God As The Mystery Of The World* (Grand Rapids MI: Eerdmans, 1983), 159.
10. Nussbaum, *Poetic Justice: The literary Imagination And Political Life*, 24.
11. John Milton, *Areopagiica*. In Abrams, 908–100.

things, asking us even in the darkest of times not to put our trust in the way things are at the moment. So the story goes that when Vita Sackville-West was asked whether she wrote about the 'real world' she replied: 'Certainly not. One of the damn things is quite enough'. At the same time, we must also hope that things as they are can be 'changed upon the blue guitar' of the imagination.

But this is not, and should not be, always a serious business. The 'golden world of the imagination' can also be playful and offer a lively and compassionate insight into the oddities of human beings, the pathos as well as into the strangeness of our eccentricities. Let me give you an example. Amos Oz is an Israeli writer of some note whose autobiography tells of growing up as the only child of Jewish migrants who arrived with little money from Poland where the family had once been well-to-do in an Israel still under British rule. It was not an easy life, especially as his parents' marriage seems to have been pretty loveless. But Oz rejoices in the ways in which, despite everything, people managed to preserve their Dignity.

One of my favourite passages is his story of his Auntie Greta, who loved going shopping and trying on clothes she could never afford to buy. His account is full of the small boy's wonder at her daring and his own anxieties:

> Auntie Greta would drag me into three or four clothes shops, in each of which she liked to try on, take off, and try on again, in the privacy of the changing cubicle, a number of beautiful dresses and a range of magnificent skirts, blouses and nightdresses, and a mass of colourful house coats that she termed negligees. Once she even tried on a fur: the look in the tortured eyes of the slain fox terrified me. The fox's face stirred my soul because it looked both cunning and heart-wrenchingly wretched.

But there is also a half-understood and-realised compassion for her:

> Time and again this broad-beamed Aphrodite was reborn from the foam, bursting from behind the curtain in a new and ever more glamorous incarnation. For my benefit and for the salesperson and other shoppers she would turn on her heel a couple of times in front of the mirror. Despite her heavy thighs she enjoyed executing a coquettish pirouette, and enquired of each of us in turn whether it suited her, whether it flattered

her, whether it clashed with the colour of her eyes, whether it hung well, didn't it make her look fat, wasn't it rather common, a bit brash? As she did so, her face reddened, and because she was embarrassed at blushing she blushed again, that deeper blood-red, verging on purple. Finally she promised the salesperson earnestly that she would almost certainly be back the same day, in fact very shortly, after lunch, by the end of the afternoon, when she'd had time just to look around some other shops, tomorrow at the latest.

So far as I can recall she never ever went back. On the contrary she was always very careful never to visit the same shop twice until several months had elapsed. Passages like this surely justify Sidney's saying that the 'poet' can have a priestly function. So Oz celebrates here his aunt's confused longings for beauty and admiration, giving us a sense of wonder and awe before the possibilities of otherwise undistinguished people.

It is time to conclude. So let us return to the idea that our present culture appears to be moving in the wrong direction and that we are losing any real sense of responsibility for it. What I have been arguing, however, is that a central task of the library is to empower the 'golden world of the imagination', to enable us to recover a sense of the wonder and awe at the possibilities implicit even in the most ordinary existence, to break out of the closed circle of one-dimensional materialism with the ability

> To see a world in a Grain of Sand,
> And a heaven in a wild flower,
> Hold Infinity in the palm of your hand
> And Eternity in an hour.

In turn this may lead us to an understanding of the ways in which our perceptions may shape the world and of our responsibilities for it, realising that, as Blake said:

> The bat that flits at close of eve
> Has left the brain that won't believe

and that

> The dog starv'd at his master's gate
> Predicts the ruin of the state.[12]

It may true that, as most of our literal-minded leaders and opinion-makers would say, writing of this imaginative kind may 'make nothing happen.' Yet in his elegy for the poet WB Yeats Auden, conceding this goes on to affirm its continuing power, that

> . . . it survives
> In the valley of its saying where executives
> Would never want to tamper . . .
> A way of happening, a mouth.[13]

---

12. Amos Oz, *A Tale Of Love And Darkness* (London: Vintage, 2005), 214.

13. WH Auden, 'In Memory Of WB Yeats', in David Daiches, *et al,* editors. *The Norton Anthology Of English Literature II*, 1962. 1626.

Are We Here But To Name The World?
Ways Of Naming And Praising The World

Let me take as my text some lines from the German poet Rainer Maria Rilke, lines which in effect echo one of the main themes of the Psalms, to give voice to the praise all creation is already giving to God:

> . . . Are we, perhaps, *here,* only to say: House,
> Bridge. Fountain. Gate. Jug. Fruit-tree. Window.—
> at most: Pillar. Tower . . . But to *say*—you understand,
> O to *say*, with an intensity the things themselves never
> hoped to achieve.[1]

Yet the Psalms also suggest that this can also be problematic. Psalm 106, for example opens with the call to 'give thanks to the Lord, for he is good; for his steadfast love endures forever.' But it follows this call with the question, 'Who can utter the mighty doings of the Lord, or declare all his praise?' Christopher Willcox's paper which we have just heard echoes a similar concern and I would like to begin with it.

Fortunately, however, he suggested an answer to the problem when he quoted the wise words of one of the sixth century bishop, advising us to 'think of what you are singing' when we praise God in the liturgy. So let us follow this advice, asking ourselves not only what we are doing but also where and when we are doing it. The answer to the first question is that we are in a place which has been named and praised for thousands of years by the First Peoples of this land and that in that sense we are carrying on that task. The answer to the second question, is more important since it is becoming increasingly

---

1. Rainer Maria Rilke, *The Duinese Elegies,* 'Ninth Elegy', in Maynard Mack *et al* (eds), *World Masterpieces* II, (New York: Norton, 1965), 1302.

evident in this country particularly that the earth and its creatures, ourselves included, are wounded. This is the result of our worship of false gods, of what I call the Unholy Trinity, Mammon, the god of money, Moloch, the god of violence and war, and McDonalds, the god of mindless and all destructive pleasures.

But what difference could the liturgy, the praise of God, make? Perhaps the best response to this question is to reflect on Ludwig Wittgenstein's observation that 'the limits of my language are the limits of my world', an observation that echoes Humpty Dumpty's 'my words are the shape I am'. If, as Jean Baudrillard argues, the mass media culture in which we live 'rests on the exaltation of signs based on the denial of the reality of things'[2]—and of people, it is a culture which is essentially superficial, often deceitful—consider the way in which words like 'democracy', 'freedom' and so on are used—and out of touch with physical reality and personal experience. Taken up into 'the ecstasy of the social',[3] we are as it were locked out of our own hearts and left with little or no ability to speak to and of the inner depths of the self.

But that is where the God whom we believe—or better perhaps, who believes in us—speaks to us, the God Karl Rahner describes as the '"silent one" who is always there, and yet can always be overlooked [and often remains] unheard, [who] because [this reality] expresses the whole in its unity and totality, can [therefore] be passed over as meaningless.'[4]

According to JB Metz the best short definition of God may therefore be interruption because the mystery of death and resurrection overturns what St Paul calls the 'wisdom of this world'. As Metz goes on to say, the marks of this revelation are love and solidarity, a memory which, unlike that of contemporary history, 'remembers not only what has succeeded, but also what has been destroyed, not only what has been achieved, but also what has been lost'.[5] In that way this kind of memory which, of course, we celebrate in the liturgy, is profoundly subversive since it 'works against the victory of what has become and already exists' by keeping alive the memory of those excluded from it. In our case it bears on our relations with the land's First Peoples since:

---

2. Jean Baudrillard, *Revenge Of The Crystal* (Sydney: Pluto Press, 1990), 63.
3. Baudrillard, *Revenge Of The Crystal,* 16.
4. Karl Rahner, *Foundations of Christian Faith* (New York: Crossroad, 1985), 46
5. Johan Baptist Metz, *Faith in History And Society* (New York: Seabury Press, 1980), 171.

> Resurrection mediated by way of the memory of suffering
> means: The dead, those already vanquished and forgotten, have
> a meaning which is as yet unrealised. The potential meaning
> of our history does not depend only on the survivors, the
> successful and those who make it. Meaning is not a category
> that is only reserved for the conquerors![6]

To return to the question of language, the language of the liturgy
therefore should, in my opinion, challenge our present commonsense
and point in the direction of realities of this kind, 'realities at present
unseen', take us to the depths of the self, the *cor secretum*. Poetry and
music are therefore essential because learning about God is 'less like
grasping an argument and more like understanding a musical theme'
which points beyond itself to the total fabric of music.[7] Close to music
as it is, this kind of language also includes gesture, the unspoken
language of the body, providing a kind of echo chamber in which
information gives way to intuition and a 'voice not our own' whose
'tone's deeper than intimate' may ask 'of us all we feared, yet longed
to say'.[8]

In this way liturgy involves the kind of 'singing Alleluia' St
Augustine writes about, a richer sense of being in the world and a
larger sense of time, not a line ceaselessly moving ahead but as the
circumference of what TS Eliot calls 'the still point of the turning
world' where past and future are gathered into the life of the Timeless
One. To refer again to the gifts traditional Aboriginal culture may
have to offer, it is worth noting that it has a similar sense of time—
something I realised listening to a friend who had been invited to
join a group of traditional people travelling out from their country
not far from Alice Springs to celebrate ceremonies with a community
across the border in western Australia. As they drove west the road
gave out and even though my friend was a good bushman he had no
idea where they were going. But his Aboriginal companions would
stop every so often, survey the country and take their bearings from
a traditional song they sang about the Dreaming hero who had made

---

6. Baptist Metz, *Faith In History And Society,* 113–114.
7. Edith Wyschogorod, *Saints and Postmodernism* (London: University of Chicago Press, 1990), 47.
8. Judith Wright, 'Poem and Audience', in *Collected Poems: 1942–1985* (Sydney: Angus & Robertson, 1994), 210.

the same journey when he came on earth. But this surely is what we Christians do—or should do—when we reflect on and celebrate the story of God's dealings with us, so that even as we move through time we are taking our directions from our Dreaming.

But referring to their wisdom in this way, I would argue, is not to turn away from revelation but to follow the logic of the God who can be seen, in the words of Eberhard Jüngel as 'the mystery of the world' whose being as far as we are concerned 'is in coming' in going 'on ways to himself through this world', even if sometimes those ways seem 'to lead to other places, even to that which is not God'.[9] This mystery of God working in and through creation is the mystery Gerard Manley Hopkins celebrates in 'Hurrahing In Harvest', a poem in which the real harvest is the glory of God:

> I walk, I lift up, I lift up heart, eyes,
> Down all that glory in the heavens to glean our Saviour . . .
>
> . . . And the azurous hung hills are his world-wielding shoulder
> Majestic—as a stallion stalwart, very-violet-sweet.[10]

But it is also the mystery we celebrate in the liturgy, especially when we read the Psalms, recognising the glory of God at work in the world and letting it speak through and in them and opening us out to its blessing.

This brings us finally to the Eucharist, the supreme work of praise in which 'the Word in person, silently, speaks and blesses, speaks to the extent that he blesses' and in which, 'eating his body and drinking his blood, [we] discover ourselves assimilated to the one whom [we] assimilate and recognise inwardly'.[11]

It is here that the synergy between 'Song, Space and Text' which we are reflecting on reaches its climax. But it is also the point at which this synergy bears most powerfully upon our world in which notions of the splendour and dignity of humanity and of creation as a whole seem to be diminishing and we are threatened with terrors created

---

9. Eberhard Jüngel, *God as The Mystery Of The World* (Grand Rapids MI: Eerdmans, 1983), 159.

10. Gerard Manley Hopkins, *Poems*, (Oxford: Oxford University Press, 1948), 74–75.

11. Jean Luc Marion, *God Without Being* (London: University of Chicago Press, 1995), 151.

by our greed, blindness and violence, in effect by our worship of false gods. A recent essay by Denis Edwards, 'Celebrating Eucharist In A Time Of Global Climate Change',[12] has some powerful things to say about the power of the Eucharist and of the ways in which it may help us develop a 'cosmic theology'.

The essay begins by referring to Pope John Paul II's Encyclical, *Gift and Mystery: On The Fiftieth Anniversary Of My Priesthood* which in turn owes a great deal to Teilhard de Chardin's *The Mass On The World* in which Chardin argues that in the Eucharist we offer 'on the altar of the whole earth the world's work and suffering' (5). This, John Paul II writes, gives us a sense of the 'universal and, so to speak, cosmic character' of the Eucharist so that 'even when it is celebrated on the humble altar of a country church, [it] is always in some way celebrated *on the altar of the world*.' But uniting heaven and earth, it interrupts our history, embracing and permeating all creation with the promise of 'the Son of Man [who] became man in order to restore all creation, in one supreme act of praise, to the one who made it from nothing . . . [T]his is the *mysterium fidei* which is accomplished by the Eucharist: the world which came forth from the hands of God the Creator now returns to him redeemed by Christ.' (5)

The present Pope [Pope John Paul II], has also written in similar vein, seeing the transubstantiated Host as the 'anticipation of the transformation and divinisation of matter in cosmos with its direction . . . [anticipating] its goal and at the same time [urging] it on' (5). At a time in which the earth is being degraded and, to quote Rilke once again,

> [m]ore than ever
> the things we live with are falling away,
> are dispossessed and replaced by an act without plan[13]

This strengthens our hope. Taking us up into the mystery of creation and redemption, it echoes the Third Eucharistic prayer's declaration that 'all creation rightly gives You praise' and intensifies its significance by joining all creation into 'cosmic companionship' with the angels and saints in their work of praise. This surely shows us even in these

---

12. Denis Edwards, 'Celebrating Eucharist In A Time Of Global Climate Change', in *Pacifica*, 19/1 (February 2006): 1–15. Page numbers will be given in my text.
13. Rilke, *The Duinese Elegies*, 1303.

dark times how splendid the world can be when even its defeats and tragedies are taken up into the triumph of the Resurrection.

As far as each of us is concerned, this gives a new intensity to the notion of the priesthood of all believers and thus new grounds of hope for and in this world. At the same time it underlines our responsibility, the task of enabling creation reach its fullness through us, to 'let all God's glory through'[14] as it flows through our lives and worship. Rilke suggests this also in the lines with which we began since the objects he singles out for praise, house, fountain, bridge, fruit-tree and so on are quite ordinary but each in its own way nurturing and expansive, making it possible for us to move on to realise more fully our 'overflowing existence'.

Nor is this merely a 'poetic' or theological conceit. Many contemporary scientists no longer see the universe as static but as an 'energy/ medium' in process of becoming.[15] They also speak increasingly and with growing respect of what is unseen and some are suggesting that the cosmos is moving in the direction of increasing consciousness and that the physical universe in this way is 'both [producing] us and, ultimately [participating] *in us* to become real'.[16] Once again this points to a synergy between song, space and text, but this time the text of creation as a whole and thus underlines the importance of the renewal of Christian worship and of the understanding that the world is in truth 'charged with the grandeur of God'[17] (17), as in Teilhard de Chardin's words,' the luminosity and fragrance which suffuse the universe take on the lineaments of a body and a face'—Christ the Lord's' (6), consecrating all of creation and of humanity by taking them up into the mystery of redemption.

The liturgy in general and the Eucharist in particular is thus the great sign of hope for our battered and suffering world and it is surely appropriate that we remember this in the weekend in which we celebrate the Ascension, *the* conclusion of the drama of the death and resurrection of the Lord of life.

---

14. Gerard Manley Hopkins, 'The Blessed Virgin Compared To The Air We Breathe', in *Poems,* 100.

15. James Studer, 'Consciousness and Reality: Our Entry Into Creation', in *Cross Currents*, 48/1 (Spring 1998): 23.

16. Studer, 'Consciousness and Reality: Our Entry Into Creation', 22.

17. Hopkins, 'God's Grandeur', *Poems,* 70.

A Forum for Theology in the World Vol 8 No 1&2/2021

Religion And The Mystery Of Beauty

Most important words are slippery things, difficult to define. But Humpty Dumpty, as so often in *Alice In Wonderland,* had some wise words to say on the subject when he observed to Alice; 'My words are the shape I am'. This is especially helpful, I think, when we are trying to discuss 'beauty' since they remind us what we are trying to talk about is not really things 'out there', a sunset, a flower, the ocean, a person's face or even a galloping thoroughbred horse, but rather our responses to these things—hence the saying that 'beauty is in the eye of the beholder.' In one way, of course, this increases our problem: what I find beautiful you may find ugly, junk, stupid or offensive. On the other hand, it helps us realise that what the word is pointing to is an experience which is deeply personal and therefore often cannot be put into words. But that surely is what makes it special. As a Danish philosopher Nicholas Stenson who lived from 1638 to 1686 wrote: 'Beautiful are the things we see. More beautiful are the things we understand. But the most beautiful are without doubt those we do not understand.'

Some people may see this as 'philosophical nonsense'. But it may be that what is unseen is at least as important, perhaps more important, than what is seen. Certainly, many contemporary scientists, physicists especially, are beginning to think that this is so. But it is also worth reminding ourselves that chapter 11 *Letter To The Hebrews* which explores the meaning and consequences of faith defines it as a 'commitment to realities at present unseen' and then goes on to define a life of faith as a journey towards the great and powerful mystery which lies at the heart of existence.

Patrick White's *Voss,* a novel inspired by the story of the nineteenth century explorer Ludwig Leichardt who died attempting to cross

Australia from east to west, echoes this idea But it also draws a contrast between those prepared to take this journey into the interior and people like the prosperous Sydney merchant Mr Bonner who long for security and cling to the fringes of the self, shrinking from what White elsewhere called 'the deep end of the unconscious',[1] as they cling to the fringes of the continent. It is true that Voss and those who remained with him died in the desert, the point White seems to be making is at the end of his story that by entering into the land the explorer has become one with the land: 'His spirit 'is there still, it is said, in the country, and always will be.'[2] What this implies, I suggest, is that living in a place is not just a matter of being there physically but of sharing in its life imaginatively—and this is surely true also of our relations with people.

Here White may or may not have had in mind in an essay by the German philosopher Martin Heidegger in which he draws a distinction between merely living and building *on* the land and dwelling *in* and *with* it, living intimately with it.[3] this may be especially important for us Australians as newcomers to a very ancient land. But perhaps we have not set ourselves properly to what another thinker, Mircea Eliade, sees as the essential task facing a people newly arrived in a place hitherto unknown to them, 'the transformation of chaos into cosmos,'[4] that is not merely to develop it materially but to find where and how we belong in it spiritually—as our Aboriginal sisters and brothers have done.

In this task our writers, musicians and visual artists have an important part to play. One of this most significant in this respect is Judith Wright who has written so powerfully about the land in poems like 'South Of My Days' about the 'clean, lean, hungry country',

with

> its . . . high delicate outline
> of bony slopes wincing under the winter,
> low trees, blue-leaved and olive, outcropping granite

---

1. Patrick White, *Flaws In The Glass* (London: Jonnathan Cape, 1981), 104.
2. White, *Flaws In The Glass,* 448.
3. Martin Heidegger, *Poetry, Language, Thought.* (New York: Harper Colophon Books, 1975).
4. Mircea Eliade, *The Myth Of The Eternal Return Or, Cosmos And History* (Princeton, Princeton University Press, 1974), 10

of the New England tableland of her childhood which has now become 'part of my blood's country'.[5]

This identification with the living world around her intensified when she was pregnant and felt herself part of its larger life. In 'Woman To Child', for example it is as if she is drawn into the mystery and power of creation itself:

> Then all a world I made in me;
> all the world you hear and see
> hung upon my dreaming blood.
>
> There move the multitudinous stars,
> and coloured birds and fishes moved.
> There swam the sliding continents.
> All time lay rolled in me,
> and love that knew not its beloved.[6]

The natural world for her, however, was always a living presence, growing up on the land, as she told an interviewer,

> I had a beautiful landscape that I loved so much and was in so much . . . Most children . . . are brought up in the 'I' tradition these days—the ego, it's me and what I think. But when you live in very close contact with a large and splendid landscape as I did you feel yourself as a good deal smaller than just I.[7]

This suggests how beauty can affect our ideas of reality and of our place within it, offering as it does a glimpse of what William Wordsworth described as

> . . . the 'burden of the mystery
> In which the heavy and the weary weight
> Of all this unintelligible world
> Is lightened . . .
> While with an eye made quiet by the power
> Of harmony, and the deep power of joy,

5. Judith Wright, *Judith Wright: Poems 1942-1983* (Sydney: Angus & Robertson, 1994), 20.

6. Wright, *Judith Wright: Poems 1942-1983*, 28.

7. Veronica Brady, *South Of My Days: A Biography Of Judith Wright* (Sydney, Angus & Robertson, 1998), 469.

We see into the life of things.
('Lines Composed Some Miles From Tintern Abbey', Abrams,
1962 76)

But it is not just a passive experience. It is also creative, enabling us to

. . . see a world in a Grain of Sand
And a heaven in a wild-flower,
Hold Infinity in the palm of your hand
And Eternity in an hour.[8]

This may seem irrelevant to the real business of life. But if you think about it, experiences of this kind, in which the way we see the world is suddenly interrupted to offer us new insights, are essential to all creativity especially perhaps in mathematics and the sciences. One physicist I know, for example, often says that he is pretty sure that such or such an equation is right because it is so beautiful—that is, so elegant. This suggests that what is beautiful may offer a glimpse beyond ourselves into the larger order of the universe. That, of course, is the message of many of the Psalms, great poems of praise like Psalm 8, Psalm 19, and Psalm 104, to name only the ones which first come to mind. Many other parts of the Bible also give us a glimpse the awesome power of this order—and the wonderful last chapters of *The Book of Job* are a good example.

So, a good way of thinking about religion may be that it rests on the belief in this mystery at the heart of existence, the mystery of the sacred which both draws us to it but also terrifies us with its splendour and power. In this country perhaps we have a special resource in traditional Aboriginal culture which has a profound sense of this mystery. In it the sacred is as it were the ground of their being, the reality in and through which they live and move which suffuses every aspect of their lives. It also includes the natural world which for them is the book in which the story of its creative power is inscribed, in the rocks and stones, the rivers, hills and plains and in the beauties of the night sky. In opening themselves to this story, reflecting on and celebrating it, they come to understand who they are and where they belong in the universe.

---

8. William Blake, *Blake, Complete Poetry And Prose,* edited by Geoffrey Keynes (London: Nonsuch Press, 1961), 118.

As we have said, most other religions share this vision. In one of his letters from prison where he was awaiting execution for his part in one of the plots to assassinate Hitler the German theologian Dietrich Bonhoeffer, for example, was sustained by the vision of the universe as one vast piece of polyphonic music in which the mysterious reality of God, the reality which St Augustine called 'the beauty ever ancient, ever new' was the base melody on which all other interweaving themes and individual melodies of our lives rested.[9]

In our culture, however many of us live with a much more limited sense of reality, more or less taking for granted the wonder of things. So it may be useful to look more closely at Aboriginal culture and ways in which it may throw light on beliefs which we may have forgotten or ignored by reflecting on a discussion between a distinguished Kimberley elder David Mowaljarlai and a sympathetic anthropologist, Jutta Malnik which they report in their Book *Yorro Yorro: Everything Standing Up Alive. Spirit Of The Kimberley.* In this particular scene they are sitting around the campfire talking about the Wanjina paintings in the caves nearby which they are to visit next day.

David was especially interested in Lejmorro, the Wanjina 'boss'. Even to see him, he told Jutta, would make her happy since he is the earthly manifestation of the Milky Way, as his name suggests: the word *lej* means 'little lights, and in connection with the Milky Way also 'lit' or 'lit from outside'. So his name implies that he is a 'light for all Aborigines' and sheds his light on others.

What his image reveals is that existence as polyphonic--in the way similar to the one Bonhoeffer described: 'Everything is represented in the ground and in the sky [David told Jutta]. You can't get away from it, because all is one, and we're in it.'[10] Our lives then are part of the life of the universe and should move according to its rhythms: 'As you sleep beside the campfire at night [he goes on] you may think you are stiff on one side and turn over; in reality, you are following the Milky Way as it turns around the earth.'

Few of us today would see the world in these terms today. But perhaps we should. Descartes' proposition, 'I think, therefore I am' implies that mind and body are separate and that we stand apart from

---

9. Dietrich Bonhoeffer, *Letters & Papers from Prison,* edited by Eberhard Bethge (New York, Simon & Schuster Touchstone Press, 1997), 303.
10. David Mowaljarlai and Jutta Malnic, *Yorro Yorro: Everything Standing Up Alive: Spirit of the Kimberley* (Broome, WA: Magabala Books, 1993), 5.

the rest of creation, operating on it, free to use it for our own ends—though the environmental crisis facing us suggests that this not be so. The sense that we a are involved in the life of creation, however was once part of Christian tradition, as of most religious traditions and in clear in Scripture. Jesus told his disciples, for instance, to learn wisdom from the birds of the air and the lilies of the field and berated his disciples for failing to understand him when he spoke in parables (which imply interlocking levels of meaning and thus reveal deeper realities). A similar view is implicit in St Paul's *Letter to the Romans* in which he sees creation as a whole involved in one great act of giving life.

A similar world view prevailed in the Middle Ages. In the *Divine Comedy*, Dante's account of a journey beginning in hell but ending in paradise, he enters heaven through an earthly paradise, nature at its most beautiful, and inspired in this way looks out across the 'great ocean' and sees all things moving, across it, each to its own way, towards ultimate reality,

> the Love that moves the sun and the other stars.
>
> (Canto XXXIII, 145)

St Francis of Assisi lived out this vision, treating all living creatures as worthy of his love as his sisters and brothers. As John Donne put it several centuries later; 'No man is an island, entire of itself; every man is a piece of the continent, a part of the main',[11] the great mainland of life.

This is not mere poetic speculation, however, as contemporary science tells us. According to Albert Einstein, for instance, we

> human beings are part of the whole which we call the Universe,
> a small region in time and space. We regard ourselves as
> separate and apart from all the rest. But this is something like
> an optical illusion . . . Our task should be to free ourselves
> from this prison, opening our circle of compassion to embrace
> all living creatures and all of nature in its beauty.[12]

As we have seen traditional Aboriginal culture also sees the world similarly, as Bonhoeffer did also when he saw reality as polyphonic rather than one-dimensional as many of us see it. It follows that there

---

11. M Abrams, *et al*, editors, *The Norton Anthology Of English Literature* (New York: Norton, 1962), 705.

12. Q Clayton, *The Dark Night Sky* (New York, Quadrangle Books, 1975), 127.

may be something fundamentally mistaken about our current ideas of reality which may in fact be damaging us as well as the environment.

In a recent novel, *Cosmopolis,* for instance, American writer Don de Lillo's central character is a typical contemporary hero, a billionaire asset manager at the age of twenty-eight. Looking out over New York, however, he finds no pleasure in what he sees or indeed who he is, only a 'great rapacious flow, where the physical will of the city, the ego fevers, the assertions of industry, commerce and crowds shape every anecdotal moment',[13] a place full of people—like him, 'lonely inside their lives', dominated by images from outside the self, a fantasy world which, in the words of Jean Baudrillard, rests on 'the exaltation of signs based on the denial of the reality of things'[14]—and, I would add, of other people—intent on acquiring more and more things and exerting power in the world rather than learning to dwell in it.

This is a meaningless world. But it does not have to be so, at least if William Blake was right when he said that in a sense the shape of the world is neither round nor flat but human-shaped, (by which he meant that the way things are depends on the way we see them). The Greeks but also the Bible and most of the great religions make a great deal of the importance of wisdom, a word derived from two Anglo-Saxon words, *wys,* the equivalent of the Greek *arête,* the perfection of a person or thing and-*dom* which describes an abiding state. So wisdom means being at home with and in the way things really are. So it follows that beauty opens the way to wisdom. That is why I see literature, music and the visual arts, which, unlike the media which deals with surfaces, ask us to enter into them and look through them into realities at present unseen. For the playwright Tom Stoppard appearances are merely 'the window-pane, the barrier, against which we press our searching face.'

If we want to change the world then we may first need to reimagine it. Theodor Adorno understood this, comparing the imagination to 'a child at the piano searching for a chord never previously heard' but knowing that, since 'the possible combinations are limited' this chord 'was always there', and therefore 'everything that can be played on it

13. Don de Lillo, *Cosmopolis* (New York: Scribner, 2003), 41.
14. Jean Baudrillard, *Revenge Of The Crystal: Essays On The Modern Object An Its Destiny, 1968-1983* (Sydney: Pluto Press, 1990), 63.

is implicitly given in the keyboard'.[15] What matters then is to keep searching. For our purposes it is significant that a child is his example here since it reminds us that most children, to begin with at least, can 'see the world in a grain of sand' and find 'eternity in an hour'. But we also need to be aware that education today often seems to damage this ability, having as its goal success in what DH Lawrence called 'the business of money-making, money-having and money-spending'. Charles Dickens foresaw this in his novel *Hard Times*. In it he contrasted the educational ideas of Mr Gradgrind—as usual with Dickens, his name tells us a good deal about him—with education which can be compared to a circus in which students enjoyed themselves, riding 'upon anything, [jumping] over everything', learning to dance and to 'stick at nothing'. A sense of beauty can offer this kind of fun. But Mr Gradgrind, proud of being 'a man of realities' Mr Gradgrind insisted on 'fact and calculation', proceeding 'upon the principle that two and two are four, and nothing over'.

A world view like this which is limited only to what we can see and touch or calculate or put in the bank can become a prison. To quote William Blake again: 'The bounded is loathed by its possessor. The same dull round, even of a universe, would soon become a mill with complicated wheels'.[16] Gerard Manley Hopkins describes this kind of a world, but also offers a way out of it, in his poem 'God's Grandeur',[17] though its title offers a way out:

> Generations have trod, have trod, have trod;
> And all is seared with trade; bleared, smeared with toil;
> And wears man's smudge and shares man's smell: the soil
> Is bare now, nor can foot feel, being shod.

But that is because we have failed to see beyond the appearances, to realise that in reality

> The world is charged with the grandeur of God.
> It will flame out, like shining from shook foil.

---

15. John Hughes, 'Unspeakable Utopia; Art And return To The Theological In Adorno And Horkheimer', in *Cross Currents*, 53/4 (Winter, 2004): 478.
16. Blake, *Blake, Complete Poetry And Prose*, 148.
17. Gerard Manley Hopkins, *Poems*, edited by WH Gardner (London: Geoffrey Cumberlege Oxford University Press, 1948), 70.

The word 'God' here might put some people off. But the comparison with foil, a metallic substance, the further comparison of the 'greatness' of this grandeur with 'the ooze of oil/ Crushed' implies that this reality does not exist 'out there' but breaks into the world of technology. Beauty and grandeur can be found anywhere if we are able to look beyond the surface appearances to the wonders contained within them. If you have ever looked at something through a microscope this will be clear. So boring or grim the appearances may seem to be, it is possible to find deeper possibilities within them.

Antoine St Exupery made this point in *The Little Prince* where he shows how an imaginative person may see what someone literal-minded would see as a drawing of a bowler hat as a boa-constrictor which has swallowed an elephant. Similarly Hopkins insists:

> There lives the dearest freshness deep down things, some power of renewal. He sees this as the work of the Spirit of the Creator brooding 'Over the bent/ World . . . with warm breast and with ah! bright wings' to bring forth new life. In their own way then the metaphors and images, like many of the stories of the sacred books of various religions and the stories indigenous peoples find inscribed in the natural world are not merely beautiful but offer insights into reality, in this case the beginnings of life as scientists describe it and all together point to the fact that, as Job acknowledged at the end of his story, we are surrounded by 'things too wonderful to me which I did not know.'[18]

So beauty cuts our ideas about ourselves down to size, reminding us of all we do not, perhaps cannot know—which is probably what Plato was getting at when he observed that the more we know, the more we realise we do not know. But if this sounds too abstract, let us say a few words also about the beauty of human beings. It emerges from what we have been saying that it is not the same thing as glamour (which the dictionary defines as 'illusory charm') but that it breaks into our everyday world to offer a glimpse into the order and splendour 'at the heart of things' and this even in otherwise apparently ordinary people.

---

18. Hopkins, *Poems,* edited by WH Gardner, *Job,* 42, 3

A passage from George Eliot's novel *Middlemarch* is a good example. It centres on Dorothea Brooke, a privileged young woman who has made a disastrous marriage—precisely because she was overawed by what she saw as the beauty of his intelligence—is coming to terms with his death. She has sat up all night thinking. But as dawn breaks she draws the curtains and looks out on the bit of road she can see beyond the gates of her estate:

> On the road there was a man with a bundle on his back and a woman carrying her baby; in the field she could see figures moving—perhaps the shepherd with his dog. Far off in the bending sky was the pearly light; and she felt the largeness of the world and the manifold wakings of men to labour and endurance. She was part of that involuntary palpitating life.[19]

This realisation is the turning point of her life. Glimpsing the dignity, courage and beauty of ordinary undistinguished women and men as they live out their lives, she is no longer alone but drawn into the community of life.

To conclude. The experience of beauty introduces us to this life in all its wonder, mystery and multiplicity. But it is not to be found in specially reserved places like art galleries or amongst specially privileged or gifted people but anywhere and in anyone at any time. All that is needed is to be open and ready to respond to its presence. That surely is important, especially today when we are surrounded with so many messages of disaster. So we conclude with lines from a poem in which Jane Graham dedicates herself to this task:

> I've begun the action of beauty again, on the burning river, I have started the catalogue, Your world.
>
> (*London Review Of Books.* 5th July, 2007)

---

19. George Eliot, *Middlemarch* (Camberwell, Vic: Penguin Classics, 1994), 788.

Bland Sacrilege In The Arts:
The Challenge of Kim Scott's Benang

As I said at last year's conference on this subject, we are engaged in an unfashionable discussion. The dictionary defines blasphemy and sacrilege as profane talk or action, an offence against what is sacred, what Rudolph Otto calls the *mysterium terribile, tremendum et fascinans* at the heart of existence to which we owe reverence and obedience.[1] But the West in general today and Australian society in particular seems to have little sense of this kind of reality. If anything, the tendency AG Stephens identified in 1905 has intensified when he wrote that 'there is in the developing Australian character a sceptical and utilitarian spirit that values the present hour and refuses to sacrifice the present for any visionary future lacking a rational guarantee.'[2] Technology which seems to allow us to dominate and control the world has intensified this refusal so that, lacking a centre outside the self and its desires, we exist in a state of 'pure circulation [in which] . . . there is no point of reference . . . and value radiates in all directions . . . without reference to anything whatsoever.'[3]

True, some would regard the growth of religious fundamentalism as a return to the sacred. But the sacred as we have defined it is a power which stands over against the self, though it may speak to and within it, whereas fundamentalism is grounded in the self, in its desires for power for power and esteem, for example, or for certainty

---

1. Rudolph Otto, *The Idea Of The Holy, An Inquiry Into The Non-Rational Factor In The Idea Of The Divine And Its Relation To The Rational.* (Oxford: Oxford University Press, 1923), 4.
2. Ian Turner, editor, *The Australian Dream* (Melbourne: Sun Books, 1969), x.
3. Jean Baudrillard, *The Transparency Of Evil*, translated by James Benedict (London: Verso, 1993), 5.

and security.[4] If this is so, the notion of blasphemy and sacrilege challenges current notions of reality and value. Yet I want to argue that a culture which lacks a sense of the sacred, of a mystery beyond the self which constitutes what Kierkegaard calls an 'Archimedean point' is in many ways deficient and destructive because at odds with what is ultimately the case.

For most traditional cultures this Archimedean point has long been established and is culturally accepted, though whether or not it is acted upon is another matter. But for settler societies like ours it needs to be discovered anew. So, Mircea Eliade argues that the 'transformation of chaos into cosmos' is the primary task and more important than economic or material development.[5] It is arguable, however, that by and large this task is still incomplete in Australia, largely for historical reasons. Captain Phillip took possession of the place not in the name of God but of the King of England. Present day Australia is thus essentially the product of the imperial history on to which, Karl Jaspers suggests there has been 'loaded a grandeur . . . stolen from God.'[6] In effect it is based on the story of Ulysses who left home and travelled through strange places but always with the intention of returning home or of turning these places into the equivalent of home,[7] making 'a new Britannia in another world', as one of the early settlers put it.[8] But this is to reject difference, to seek to destroy or assimilate it, establishing in effect a 'closed circle around sameness.'[9]

Its notion of good and evil, which according to Levinas constitutes the 'first philosophy'[10] is, however, limited one since, as Luiz Carlos Susin argues, it defines good and evil 'in a very particular way based on itself, on its glorious position as basis and referent of all of reality

---

4. This, of course, is the substance of Marx's critique of religion in general in the Introduction to *Toward A Critique Of Hegel's Philosophy Of Law*.
5. Mircea Eliade, *The Myth Of The Eternal Return Or, Cosmos And History* (Princeton: Princeton University Press, 1975), 10.
6. Lotte Kohler and Hans Saner, editors. *Correspondence Hannah Arendt Karl Jaspers 1926-1969* (New York: Harcourt Brace, 1992), 145.
7. Luiz Carlos Susin, 'A Critique Of The Identity Paradigm', in *Concilium*, 2 (2002): 87.
8. William Charles Wentworth, inn Ian Turner editor, *The Australian Dream* (Melbourne: Sun Books, 1969), 12.
9. Susin, 'A Critique Of The Identity Paradigm', 87.
10. Sean Hand, editor, *The Levinas Reader* (Oxford: Wiley-Blackwell, 1993), 82.

spread out at its feet'.[11] The result is that it has little or no ability to relate to, much less feel for, the other/Other. A Dirk Moses makes this point in his review of Bain Attwood's *Telling The Truth About Aboriginal History:*

> A priori, settler Australians have no reason to care about indigenous experiences. Even if they acknowledge Aboriginal suffering, they engage in a simple moral calculus . . . any injustice that has been committed is redeemed by the just nature of the modern society that replaced the indigenous ones.[12]

The parallel between this passage and what Hannah Arendt has to say about Germany in the 1930s, however, is troubling:

> [E]vil in the Third Reich had lost the quality by which people recognise it, the quality of temptation. Many Germans . . . must have been tempted not to murder, not to rob, not to let their neighbours go off to their doom, and not to become accomplices in all these crimes by benefiting from them. But, God knows, they had learned to resist temptation.[13]

According to Levinas the ethical and the ontological are two sides of the one reality since existence is not monolithic but pluralist: 'We recognise the other as resembling us, but exterior to us; the relationship with the other is a relationship with a Mystery.' But this Mystery is something we cannot master. It stands irreducibly there. But so too, Levinas argues, with the other since its entire being as far as we are concerned is 'constituted by its exteriority, or rather its alterity, for exteriority is a property of space'. That, he concludes, is why it 'leads the subject back to itself through light',[14] the light of being itself which stands over against the enclosure of the self. In effect then it is the relationship with the other which makes us properly human, that is, open and compassionate.

---

11. Susin, 'A Critique Of The Identity Paradigm', 80.
12. A Dirk Moses, 'Provincialism', in *Australian Book Review,* 276 (November, 2005): 14.
13. Claire Elise Katz, 'The Problem Of Evil And The Question Of Responsibility', in *Cross Currents,* 55/2 (Summer 2005): 215.
14. Hand, *The Levinas Reader,* 43.

To return for the moment to Dirk Moses, this understanding seems to me implicit when he writes that if settler Australians are to get outside the moral calculus which prevents them from feeling for and with Aboriginal Australians 'they need to be moved by stories of [their] and believe them to be true.' Similarly, 'If historians are to promote moral Consciousness . . . regarding the value of alterity, they need to master a certain rhetoric and emotional register . . rather than engage in theoretical parlour games.'[15] That is why the arts may have an important part to play since they exist in the hypothetical mode, challenging matter-of-fact by offering new possibilities and injecting 'a core of meaning beneath the platitude of immediate physical presence'[16] or of the frame of our present culture. As Sir Philip Sidney argued in his 'Apology For Poetry', other forms of knowledge more or less deal with what is already the case. Only poetry, by which he means the arts in general, 'disdaining to be tied to any such subjection . . . doth grow in effect another nature, in making things either better . . . or quite new',[17] take us beyond the 'closed circle around sameness' and enable us to feel for and with the other.

Let us turn then to look at a recent work of fiction, Kim Scott's novel *Benang*, which does that, gives an account of the story of the settlement of south eastern Western Australia through the eyes of its Aboriginal inhabitants. Significantly, however, Scott himself has a foot in both camps, having been brought up as part of mainstream white society but having discovered recently that is a descendant of the Nyoongar people of the area. His central character and the novel's narrator, Harley, who tells their story is exploring his own newly discovered identity. But he is also interrogating ours. As the 'first-born-successfully-white-man-in-the-family-line',[18] the result of his grandfather's conclusion that the only way to survive to 'breed out' their 'blackness' and turn his descendants into whites, he also functions as our mirror image, 'an imaginary figure who at the same time causes us 'to be [ourselves] while at the same time never seeming

---

15. Moses, 'Provincialism', 14.

16. Pierre Levy, *Becoming Virtual: Reality In The Digital Age* (New York: Plenum Trade, 1998), 16.

17. MH Abrams *et al*, editors, *The Norton Anthology Of English Literature*, I (New York: WW Norton, 1962), 426.

18. Kim Scott, *Benanag* (Fremantle: Fremantle Arts Centre Press, 1999), 22. Hereafter all page references will be given in the text of the essay.

like [ourselves]'[19] and thus involves us in the story of settlement seen from the other side of the frontier.

It is a grim story of dispossession, murders, rapes, imprisonment and humiliation which interrogates and in a sense blasphemes against the pieties of the official history of settlement, setting it in the context of personal experience and in this way suggesting that historical events cannot be justified by 'referring to some abstract and anonymous law' or supposed divine or historical sanction but must be judged by its effect on others. Judged in this way, it appears that our 'place in the sun', our possession of this country meant, as Levinas puts it, writing of recent Western culture generally, 'the usurpation of spaces belonging to the other . . . whom [we] have . . . oppressed or starved, or driven out into a third world.'[20]

This dispossession is *Benang's* subject. Its ethical basis, however, reaches beyond that of imperial history which rests on material success or failure, being an ethic of responsibility, the assumption it that in the larger scheme of things the meaning of human existence does not depend only on the 'winners' and that the 'losers', 'the dead, those already vanquished and forgotten' may have a meaning yet to be realised.[21] This makes *Benang* an uncomfortable book since it breaks the taboo, the defence against the 'peril of the Soul . . . in the presence of things that are forbidden to profane experience [and] . . . cannot be approached without risk when one is not ritually prepared',[22] which protects us against awareness of the Aboriginal side of our history.

But the novel is also doubly blasphemous since it questions our notions of reality. Harley is a figure of fantasy as well as of history and thus exists on a 'level in which simultaneous estrangement from himself and intimacy with himself are played out'[23]—something which mocks our monolithic sense of identity. He also parodies the identity imposed on him as an Aborigine, remarking early in his story that '[i]t was terrible to see the shapes, the selves, I took'; now a romantic figure, 'motionless against a setting sun; posture perfect, brow noble, features fine', now a drunk, 'slumped, grinning, furrow-browed, with

19. Baudrillard, *The Transparency Of Evil*, 113.
20. Hand, *The Levinas Reader*, 82.
21. Johann Baptist Metz, *Faith In History And Society: Toward A Practical Fundamental Theology* (New York: Seabury Press, 1980), 113–114.
22. Paul Ricoeur, *The Symbolism Of Evil* (Boston: Beacon Press, 1969), 123.
23. Baudrillard, *The Transparency Of Evil*, 113.

a bottle in my hand', now a cowboy or boxer or footballer, or a 'tiny figure, sprawled on the ground in some desert place, dying' (14). This, of course, points to the ways in which we refuse to allow others their own identity but impose our perceptions on them.

The novel also attacks the policy of assimilation, of taking children away from their families, trying to destroy their culture and so on, which was justified by the claim that it was intended, in the words of A O Neville, Chief Protector of Aborigines in Western Australia, to 'uplift and elevate these people to our own plane', by having Harley parody it by claiming to have a remarkable 'propensity for elevation', a tendency to float upwards, which he constantly does, both indoors and outdoors. This parody, however, has a serious intention. One passage especially indicates the blasphemous nature of this project, the way in which people were robbed of their identity and dignity and turned into mere objects of manipulation. It shows Harley's grandfather Ern and Sergeant Hall, the local policeman and thus the official 'Protector of Aborigines', discussing Ern's suggestion that Hall might marry one of the women in Ern's family:

> They spoke of breeding and uplifting. These two hairy angels wished to seize people in their long arms and haul them to their own level. Their minds held flickering images of canvas Ascensions, with fat, pale cherubs, spiralling upwards, into the light. They saw steps leading up stone pyramids, and realised that some creatures were simply unable to continue higher, though the steps were there for them. Their noble selves sat at the top . . . Those hairy angels, scratching at their groins. Belching. Drinking beer (77).

The irreverence is devastating, and its target notions of racial superiority. But the trope of elevation also echoes a notion of the sacred common to many indigenous peoples, in the image of magical flight which is associated with the comprehension of secret sacred things and expresses the belief that some transformation, even some ontological mutation has occurred in the person him/herself.[24] Seen in this light Harley's propensity could also be seen as a critique of the superficial weightlessness and de-centeredness of Western culture

---

24. Mircea Eliade, *Symbolism, The Sacred And The Arts* (New York: Crossroad, 1990), 4.

and an assertion of belief in the sacred. Certainly, for him there is nothing sacred about the imperial story. It is merely a 'bad smell' (10), not only of the Aboriginal dead but also of the 'anxiety, of anger and betrayal' (11) which followed.

In effect this story ignores the 'otherworldly' aspect of the ethical, the obligation to respond to the claims of the take-into-account the claims of the other whose 'face summon me, calls for me, begs for me . . . [and] calls me into question' precisely because of its 'pure otherness', and is thus able to sustain what Levinas describes as a 'murderous uprightness'.[25] To the extent that they are unable to recognise that 'there is . . . another "other" at the heart of the self [to be found] in the form of ethical obligation',[26] however, *Benang* is able to present the settlers as barely human, humanity since humanity, it is implied, depends in large measure on compassion. This is clear in the scene in which the police capture an Aboriginal and hang him under the approving eyes of a group settlers while from the reserve his own people, a 'little troupe', watch helplessly in the gathering dusk. The doubling effect works powerfully here. Noticing the black onlookers, the whites see them as a 'circus . . . A zoo. A bloody freak show' and despise the poverty of the reserve, 'a few rough shelters and a small house and stable' (332). But the drift of the passage and of the novel as a whole suggests that what they see is in fact the mirror image of themselves 'the shadow . . . which haunts the subject as his "other"'.[27]

From our account so far it seems that the novel's approach is merely negative, a story of suffering and defeat. But there is also a positive aspect, implicit in the title: 'Benang' means 'tomorrow' and it is the last word of the novel's last sentence: 'We are still here, Benang' (497). What is implied, I suggest, is that the 'closed circle around sameness' of imperial culture, its 'totalisation of identity' must break up. In the glimpses the novel offers of Aboriginal culture, it points to a larger, more ultimate sense of reality and value. The account it gives of the brutalities of settlement is an account of what Levinas calls 'the evil of being' whose 'suffocating presence' we must endure if we are to become aware of and accept that 'Being is essentially strange'.[28]

---

25. Hand, *The Levinas Reader*, 82.
26. Hand, *The Levinas Reader*, 83.
27. Baudrillard, *The Transparency Of Evil*, 113.
28. Baudrillard, *The Transparency Of Evil*, 90.

It is this Other which stands over against the culture intent on domination and control the novel describes and does violence to it—which is why it provokes an answering violence. Judith Wright understood this when she describes her settler grandfather pondering the fate of the Aboriginal people he and the other settlers had dispossessed and realising that in effect they had said to us newcomers: 'you must understand us or you must kill us'. They were unable to give up their culture and their identity because it bound them irrevocably not merely to a specific place or time but to the life of the cosmos. But for the settlers this 'understanding would have meant some renunciation impossible to be made'[29] since it asked them to surrender the exclusive power and possessions they claimed for themselves to acknowledge a power beyond themselves, the power of the sacred.

Because they have made this acknowledgement, *Benang* suggests, in the long run the Aboriginal peoples will survive. Their conquerors' is an 'identity *chez-soi* or for-itself'.[30] But theirs is open, in tune with the cosmos rather than with history. It is this attunement which, despite the grim story he has to tell sustains Harley. For the settlers the land they occupy it is merely an empty stage on which to play out their dreams of power and possession. But for him and his people it is a living presence which speaks to and through him, something he has not lost, even if he has become the 'first-white man born'. So his self is not solitary, nor is the story he has to tell: '[I]t is not really *me* who sings, for . . . through me we hear the rhythm of many feet pounding the earth, and the strong pulse of countless hearts beating', (9) celebrating the mystery of existence in tune with the rest of creation, listening to 'the creak and rustle of various plants in various winds, the countless beatings of different wings, the many strange and musical calls of animals who have come from this place right here' (9–10).

That is why, despite everything, *Benang* concludes on a triumphant note:

> Speaking from the heart I tell you I am part of a much older
> story, one of a perpetual billowing from the sea, with its

29. Judith Wright, *The Generations Of Men* (Melbourne: Oxford University Press, 1965), 163.
30. Susin, 'A Critique Of The Identity Paradigm', 88.

> rhythms of return, return, and remain. Even now we gather, on chilly evenings, sometimes only a very few of us, sometimes more. We gather our strength in this way. From the heart of all of us. Pale, burnt and shrivelled, I hover in the campfire smoke and sing as best I can. I am not alone (497).

The colonial self is monolithic. But the indigenous culture it attempts to overcome is multiple and in that sense, it is implied, indestructible. Throughout the colonising culture appears as destructive, not only of people but of the natural world. But as the novel concludes it throws out a challenge which is also partly a threat:

> I offer these words, especially to those of you I embarrass, and who turn away from the shame of seeing me; or perhaps it is because your eyes smart as the wind blows the smoke a little towards you, and you hear something like a million million many-sized hearts beating, and the whispering of waves, leaves, grasses. We are still here, Benang (497).

To sum up. Seen from the point of view of the Aboriginal other, in which everything that lives is holy, non-indigenous Australian culture can be seen as blasphemous. For it the world is not the creation of human history or technology but of unseen presences with whom they cooperate. Reality therefore is not closed in on itself. Everything holds together in a system of correspondences and resonances.

Border, Identity And
The Question Of Australia

Though it may refer to physical features—the fact that Australia is 'girt by sea', for example—a border is in fact an imaginative construct, part of the construction of the 'imagined community' which is called a 'nation'. It can have both negative and positive connotations; as a mark of separation or, if used as a verb, the action of approaching or verging on another culture or environment. As it has been defined in this country since its beginnings as a settler society, however, it has usually been defined negatively as an expression and focus of anxiety about invasion from outside but also of subversion from within: witness the fear of 'the Yellow Peril', the White Australia Policy, attempts to destroy Aboriginal cultures, recent events at Cronulla, the treatment of asylum seekers, and so on.

Most settler societies, I suppose, belong to what Walter Benjamin has called the 'tradition of catastrophe', they originated at a crucial moment of cultural disruption, a loss of faith in some of its certainties—by those involved in emigrating at least—and the acceptance of a need for change. This displacement, however, made for the kind of anxiety described in Henry Kingsley's *the Recollections of Geoffrey Hamlyn*. First comes 'the disturbance of household gods, and the rupture of life-old associations' with the realization that, as Hamlyn put it, he was going 'to a land where none know me or care for me, [leaving] forever all that I know and love. Few know the feeling . . . of isolation, almost of terror, at having gone so far out of the bounds of ordinary life; the feeling of self-distrust and cowardice at being alone and friendless in the world, like a child in the dark.'[1]

---

1. JSD Mellick, editor, *Portable Australian Authors: Henry Kingsley* (St Lucia, QLD: University of Queensland Press, 1982), 134–135.

As one sociologist points out, identity here echoes the story of Ulysses, the hero who left home and travelled through strange and dangerous places, but always with the intention of returning home— as Hamlyn does, having redeemed the family fortunes in Australia— or of transforming these places into the equivalent of home,[2] building 'a new Britannia in another world' as one early settler put it.[3] But, as Susin says, this 'Odyssey of the West' was 'not an authentic adventure . . . [but] a closed circle around sameness'[4] in which difference is seen as threatening, to be destroyed or assimilated and good and evil is defined in terms of the imperial self which, seen 'as basis and referent of the whole of reality spread out at its feet'.[5] If this is seen as the pattern underlying our society the present concern with establishing and defending borders is not surprising.

What we are dealing with, however, largely exists at the unconscious level and is mostly a matter of implicit assumption rather than explicit statement. Fiction can be a useful way of exploring these assumptions, to the extent that it uses symbolic rather than literal description: symbols, as Paul Ricoeur argues, provide access to the unconscious, to what is otherwise unspoken and often unspeakable since it belongs to the dimension of 'the archaic, the nocturnal, the oneiric'[6] and can thus function 'as surveyor's staff and guide' for understanding.[7] So I want to examine two recent works, Andrew Mc Gahan's *The White Earth* and Kate Grenville's *The Secret River*, one of which explores the current preoccupation with borders, both external and internal, and the other is looking to move across them.

To consider it first, the central character in Mc Gahan's novel, John McIvor, sees the world as a dark and dangerous place where evil lurks, threatening his security and possessions. This sense permeates the novel. Its opening image, for instance, is catastrophic, a dark cloud which 'rolled and boiled as it climbed into the clear blue day, casting a vast shadow upon the hills beyond' and is compared to the mushroom

---

2. Luiz Carlos Susin, 'A Critique of The Identity Paradigm', in *Concilium*, 2 (2000): 78–90.
3. WC Wentworth, in Ian Turner, editor, *The Australian Dream* (Melbourne: Sun Books, 1968), 12.
4. Susin, 'A Critique of The Identity Paradigm', 87.
5. Susin, 'A Critique of The Identity Paradigm', 80.
6. Paul Ricoeur, *The Symbolism of Evil* (Boston: Beacon Press, 1969), 348
7. Ricoeur, *The Symbolism of Evil*, 13.

cloud of a nuclear explosion.[8] In fact its cause, the explosion of a harvester which kills a farmer, and metaphorically at least, it does mark the end of his previous world for the boy who witnesses it, William, McIvor's nephew since his father was that farmer. This melodramatic image sets the tone for the rest of the novel.

Melodrama, the conflict between absolute good and absolute evil, tends to arise within the 'closed circle around sameness.' *The White Earth*'s tone is melodramatic, full of apocalyptic images like this. Mc Ivor, a dark repressive figure who dominates the novel, has overtones of Heathcliff in *Wuthering Heights,* though without his erotic appeal. A self-made, he believes he is beholden to no one'. But he is also typical 'imperial self', not concerned, as those who belong to traditional societies are to find his place in the world but rather determined to remake that world to his own image. When it seems to be going in a direction he dislikes, when the Government moves to legislate for Aboriginal Land Rights, for instance, he founds a Movement and then organises a rally to oppose it.

Its Charter is about defending Australia's borders and the 'White Man's Supremacy', on the one hand rejecting 'the United Nations and any other body that seeks to limit Australian sovereignty' and on the other attacking 'preferential treatment of elite minorities' (by which McIvor, like Pauline Hanson in real life, largely identifies with Aboriginal Australians). The Charter proclaims his belief in 'One Flag, One People, One Nation' (133)—a slogan which echoes Hitler's 'One Land, One Law, One People' (133). Underlying this is that the land is ours by right of conquest, in effect that might equals right and that dissent and difference must be suppressed.

Seen from the outside, however, this view is the product not only of ethical poverty but also of the historical ignorance. Mere assertion like Mc Ivor's that 'the Aborigines were gone and wouldn't be coming back' (p.100) is no proof that this is so. Indeed the narrative suggests that it is not, suggesting, as we will see, that Mc Ivor is haunted by their continuing presence as well as by talk of Land Rights. Even his declaration to members of his Movement—'This is my property now. This is all your properties, your farms, your houses, your yards . . . We must be prepared to defend what we own . . . Australia—every

---

8. Andrew McGahan, *The White Earth*. Sydney (Sydney: Allen & Unwin, 2004), 1. All page references hereafter given in my text.

square inch of it—it is *our* sacred site' (209)—bespeaks their presence. In fact this assertion sit uneasily with his claim that he is defending 'the inherent value of Australian culture and traditions' since that culture and traditions necessarily includes those of the First Peoples who have inhabited this land from time immemorial. But in Mc Ivor's mind history belongs only to the 'winners', people like himself, and has no place for 'losers'.

Yet these assertions, the novel suggests, are the product of personal anxiety, even at the social level where he seems to have succeeded. As the owner of Kuran, the station which originally belonged to a pioneering family, he is an usurper. His father had been the manager but had brought up his son to believe that one day he would take over the station by marrying the daughter of the family, their only child. But when his approaches are contemptuously dismissed, he sets himself to succeed by his own efforts, working obsessively to get the money do so and sacrificing everything, including his marriage, in the process.

To use a distinction made by Helene Cixous[9] this obsession with property is essentially 'masculine'—in contrast with the culture she calls 'feminine, which is open, ready to give and receive from others, is less preoccupied with external than with inner reality, with 'the resonance of fore-language', what is unspoken and often unconscious and is thus prepared to move across borders rather than defend them. McIvor, however, is perpetually on the defensive, determined to rely only on himself. As Cixous observes, in the 'masculine' economy, 'the moment you receive something you are effectively 'open' to the other, [but] if you are a man, you have only one wish, and that is hastily to return the gift, to break the circuit of an exchange that could have no end . . . to be nobody's child, to owe no one a thing'[10]—and I do not need, I think, to spell out the parallels with the policies of our present Government and the beliefs of its supporters.

Significantly, however, as the novel draws to its end, Mc Ivor's nephew is beginning to move in the opposite, 'feminine', direction, increasingly open to the 'fore-language' of the land first of all as he explores Kuran and senses in it 'something powerful in its own

---

9. Toril Moi, *Sexual/Textual Politics: Feminist Literary Theory* (London: Routledge, 1991), 110–113.

10. Moi, *Sexual/Textual Politics,* 112.

right—to hear a voice in it, meant specifically for human ears' (100). But this voice also introduces him to a history different from the one which sustains his uncle which is about heroic explorers and pioneers, shepherds and stockmen, bush rangers and Diggers and so on. It suggests another set of images of 'deranged things, wrong things' (327) to do with the Aboriginal story. It speaks especially loudly at the spring from which, significantly, the main river system of the country originates, but into which in the past the bodies of the Aboriginal owners of Kuran murdered by settlers had been thrown. The boy senses here smell 'of blood and death . . . something invisible which made the air too potent to breathe . . . some cold and ancient secret of the land itself' (326) and begins to realize that should his uncle make him his heir the ownership of Kuran would prove 'no gift . . .[but] a burden' (327).

The contrast between him and his uncle is drawn here and the narrative comes down on Williams'. Not long after the violent collapse of his Movement Mc Ivor dies in the fire which consumes the decaying mansion, the Kuran homestead—a properly melodramatic ending, of course, in which the 'baddie' is destroyed. For our present purposes, however, it is worth noting that the lurid description of him as a thing of terror also has him turn his head 'slowly, searching, just as it had been searching the first time William had seen it' (367). Perhaps this is to suggest that the other side of the frontier he has drawn so firmly cannot be denied.

The other work I want to explore—though for lack of time only briefly—*The Secret River,* takes us into this country, suggesting a positive definition of 'border' not as a place where the other is rejected but where a new exchange may begin. There is also a personal urgency in this novel since its central character is loosely based on the figure of Grenville's great-great-great-grandfather and had its beginnings at the Walk for Reconciliation across the Harbour Bridge in 2000 when the novelist's eyes met those of an Aboriginal woman who smiled at her. 'In that instant of putting my own ancestor together with this woman's ancestor', she writes, 'everything swivelled: the country, the place, my sense of myself in it.' Walking across the bridge 'we were strolling towards reconciliation—what I had to do was cross the hard way, through the deep water of our history.'[11]

---

11. Kate Grenville, *Searching For The Secret River* (Melbourne: Text Publishing, 2006), 13.

Reimagining the story of her ancestor, whom she calls William Thornhill, Grenville explores the beginnings of division, attempting to understand rather than to blame. Her ancestor, a poor man transported for life for stealing, belongs to the 'tradition of catastrophe', a victim of the system but also in the long run its beneficiary since it enables him to take up land, displacing its Aboriginal owners and finally involving him in a massacre to destroy their resistance. Illiterate and at bay before the strangeness of this place, he has inherited the prejudices of his culture. The novel is not interested in Manichean notions of good and evil, however but in the way out of the cul de sac in which we find ourselves. My time is running out and this conclusion is only hinted at. So I can only look briefly at two key scenes.

The first tries to sum up what really happened when Thornhill went to the native camp to order them to leave, invoking English notions of property, telling them; '*This mine now.*' Thornhill's *place*. But this is not England and English law, like the English language means nothing to his hearers and his words flow past them 'as if they mattered as little as a current of air'.[12] As for Thornhill 'the Aboriginal presence is a hollow . . . a space of difference.[13] Neither side understands the other and so the encounter foreshadows the violence by which the impasse is resolved.

> A conversation had taken place. There had been an inquiry and an answer.
> But what inquiry, which answer?
> They stared at each other, their words between them like a wall (197).

The question then is how the wall might be breached so that we will not be swept along as Thornhill was by the current of violence.

The novel's conclusion suggests a possible answer as Thornhill, now an old man, sits at sunset to watch the light on the cliffs opposite blazing gold even after the dusk had left 'them glowing secretively with an after-light that came from the rocks themselves' (334). The cliffs are a wall. But something glimmers there in them which, it is implied, will lead him through them into the land itself where he

---

12. Kate Grenville, *The Secret River* (Melbourne: Text publishing, 2005), 196. All page references hereafter given in my text.
13. Grenville, *Searching For The Secret River*, 199.

senses still the Aboriginal presence. There is no time to spell out what this may signify. But what seems to me to be clear that now he is beginning to be open to the other. What this might mean was suggested by Levinas:

> It is in the laying down by the ego of its sovereignty (in its 'hateful' modality) that we find ethics and also probably the very spirituality of the soul, but most certainly the meaning of being, that is, its appeal for justification.[14]

---

14. Sean Hand, editor, *The Levinas Reader* (Oxford: Wiley-Blackwell, 1993), 85.

Called By The Land To Enter The Land

Every human being, to a greater or lesser extent, lives between worlds, between belonging and alienation. But for a variety of reasons, historical and geographical, this is especially true for non-Aboriginal Australians. In this essay, then, I would like to explore one particular aspect of our situation, our relations with the land which are summed up in its title; first of all in the double meaning of the word 'land' as it is used here but also in the implications of the word 'called', in itself a kind of profession of faith that reality is not one-dimensional but polyphonic and even dialogical, and that each of us and each creature has a part to play in the cosmic dance, a self to fulfill and to be.

This implies that the first task is to listen, to be attentive to and obey the call we hear—the word 'obedience' derives from the Latin verb 'to hear'. But it is important also to insist on the particularity of the call which comes to us as members of a specific culture and community but also as individuals in a particular place at a particular moment in history. So let me reflection the way the call comes to me as a non-indigenous Australian whose forbears came here from the other side of the world relatively recently, whereas Aboriginal Australians whose ancestors have lived here in tune with tune with the land for at least 30,000 years. Our misunderstanding of them and their culture may therefore be a crucial problem.

At a conference I attended some years ago an incident happened which made me aware of this, though in an indirect way, as a kind of parable. It happened at night in the residential College where most of us were staying and were asleep. One of us, a keynote-speakers, an Aboriginal leader, however, had been out and when he returned found himself locked out with nobody about to let him in. Unable to rouse anyone, he walked around the building to see what could be done and outside the kitchen door caught sight of the rubbish bins and dragged one of them to a place directly underneath his room. Then, standing on it, his idea was to pull himself up to a balcony next to it. In the process he fell several times into the bushes, which broke his fall. Nobody heard the noise, however, and we all slept on undisturbed. Eventually, however, he managed to reach the balcony, swung himself across to his window sill, then climbed through the open window into his room. And settled down for the night

When he told the story the next morning, I realised it was a kind of parable. Here we were newcomers have taken over the building in which he and his people have lived since time immemorial and left him outside without a key. Yet he knew how to get in and make himself at home again while we were asleep. Perhaps, then, we need to wake up to what they (who have lived here so successfully) may have to say to us, and learn from them what the land they know so intimately may be saying to us, and how urgent its message is. In the short time we have been living here we have devastated some of its most fertile areas, imposing on it crops it is unaccustomed to bear, introducing animals whose hard hooves have broken up the precious topsoil which has then blown away on the wind and chopping down vast areas of forest which has reduced rainfall and increased the salination of the soil. Our cities and technological culture have also poisoned the atmosphere, also affecting the climate.

Nearly seventy years ago the poet Judith Wright (who had grown up not only on but also with the land) realised what was happening. A poem she wrote during the long drought in the late 1940s, 'Dust', describes 'sick dust, spiraling with the wind' blowing across once fertile land as:

> [t]he remnant earth turns evil,
> the steel-shocked earth has turned against the plough.

But looking back to the prosperous times when

> [l]eaning in our doorway together
> watching the bird cloud shadows,
> the fleet wing wind shadow travel our clean wheat
> we thought ourselves rich already.
> We counted the beautiful money

she realises why this has happened:

> . . . Our dream was the wrong dream,
> our strength was the wrong strength.

It was strength we pitted against the land, attempting to conquer it instead of learning to love it and move to its rhythms. The way forward, then, was not more action but more intuition:

> Weary as we are, we must make a new choice,
> a choice more difficult than resignation . . .
> . . . We must prepare the land for a difficult sowing,
> a long and hazardous growth of a strange bread,
> That our son's sons may harvest and be fed.[1]

For the rest of her career she was looking for this change of heart, convinced that the state of the land is a reflection of our values. But this, she insisted, meant that the solution is in our hands:

> . . . [W]e know only ourselves
> have choice or power to make us whole again;
> time lifts no knives to heal or to destroy,
> and did not cause, and cannot cure, our pain ('Waiting', *CP*, 10).

But it is a choice which depends on awareness—to revert to our parable, on awakening from the dream of power and of the separation of self and world which we have been living out, realising that the land is not a mere resource to be exploited but 'part of [our] blood's country' ('South Of My Days', *CP*, 20). She also believed that the land's First Peoples, 'ourselves writ strange' ('Nigger's Leap', *CP*, 15). whose wisdom we have ignored, to our cost and that of the land, much to teach us.

From the early days of settlement, many of our writers, poets especially, have been drawn in this way to the land. Perhaps the classic statement was made by Joseph Furphy in *Such Is Life* published in 1903. 'It is not in our cities or townships, it is not in our agricultural or mining areas [he wrote] that the Australian attains full consciousness of his [or her]nationality' but in the interior. It is here, he argued, that we will find an 'unconfined, un-gauged potentiality of resource', an 'ideographic prophecy . . . a latent meaning' inscribed in the land which it is our task to decipher 'faithfully and lovingly.'[2]

---

1. Judith Wright, 'Dust', *Collected Poems of Judith Wright 1942-1985* (Sydney: Angus & Robertson, 1994), 23–4. Henceforth all references will be given in my text are from this collection and shortened to *CP*.
2. John Barnes, editor, *Portable Australian Authors: Joseph Furphy* (St Lucia, Qld: Queensland University Press, 1981), 65.

By and large, however, as we have been suggesting, we have not been able to do this, clinging to the fringes of the continent and of ourselves, unable to come to terms with the land and Aboriginal Australia, trying to impose our values on them to build 'a new Britannia in another world'[3]—as one early settler, William Charles Wentworth, put it—living in what has been described as a 'closed circle around sameness. Perhaps this is why under the apparently cheerful surface there is a sadness in our culture, a suspicion of enthusiasm, an irony which is usually self-irony, emotionally asleep as it were in the land we have occupied.

If we accept the distinction Helene Cixous draws[4] between a 'masculine' and a 'feminine' way of being in the world, it becomes clear that this is a 'masculine' culture, one which lives by the 'Economy of the Proper', preoccupied with property, propriety and appropriation and suspicious of difference and the other/Other. But by and large Aboriginal Australia lives by a 'feminine' economy, what Cixous calls the 'Economy of the Gift', open and receptive, giving and receiving from the other and living from within. Attuned to 'the resonance of fore-language . . . the language of 1,000 tongues which knows neither enclosure nor death', the mysterious language of the earth, it moves beyond mere rational understanding and calculation to an awareness of the sacred, a *mysterium tremendum et facinans* at the heart of existence something which the Enlightenment culture we have newcomers have brought with us finds it difficult to do.

Our history therefore, as someone has remarked, has thus largely represented a 'quest for normality' and a shrinking from the uncanny[5] and the transformative possibilities it offers. So the mysteriously powerful centre of the continent is seen as 'the Dead Heart of Australis', echoing the response of the nineteenth century explorer Captain Sturt. 'The Captain feels most dreadfully chagrined [one of his party wrote]. The scene is the climax of desolations; no trees, no shrubs, all bleak, barren, undulating sand. Miserable! Horrible!' As Sturt himself said it as a 'country not to be understood'.[6] Therefore, it

---

3. Ian Turner, editor, *The Australian Dream* (Melbourne: Sun Books, 1968), 12.
4. The best short account of the work of Helene Cixous is to be found in Toril Moi, *Sexual/Textual Politics* (London, Routledge, 1991), 108–126.
5. John Kinsella's recent essay, 'An Uncanny Reading Of A D Hope's "The Death Of The Bird"', *Southerly*, 68/3 (2008): 172–187. It also refers to Ken Gelder and Jane Jacob's book length study, *Uncanny Australia*.
6. Dick Smirth, 'Dick Smith's Journey Of Discovery And Adventure', *Australian Geographic*, 1 January/March (1986): 36.

was lacking in value since the Book of Nature here seemed closed, the mere 'scribblings of Nature learning to write', to quote Marcus Clarke who therefore found its dominant note to be a 'Weird Melancholy'.[7]

But to return to Furphy and Wright who represent a different, 'feminine', intuitively receptive strain, they were prepared to respond to the call of the land, Furphy tentatively, but Wright much more clearly since she was more aware of and open to Aboriginal Australia. This brings me back to my parable. The people we have largely locked out from the country to which they belonged may actually have the key to living in it properly. This is a way which includes the 'feminine', no longer sets the self over against the land but relates intimately with it. Kakadu elder, the late Bill Neidjie, for example, summed up the relationship in this way:

> Listen carefully this, you can hear me.
> I'm telling you because earth just like mother
> and father and brother of you.
> That tree, same thing.
> Your body, my body, I suppose.
> I'm same as you . . . anyone.
> Tree working when you sleep or dream.[8]

To conclude, then, if we are to live properly in this land we have much to learn from those who have done so for so long and successfully. This will entail a radical new way of thinking about ourselves and of our place in the scheme of things, perhaps even the 'long and hazardous growth of a strange bread' Judith Wright spoke of. Nevertheless, I would argue that the evidence suggests that we may need, as Stephen Muecke writes, to build 'a new house in which the spirit can more comfortably reside'. As he goes on to point out, this 'may mean leaving home and getting lost for a while, to admit that there may not be a road going anywhere that we all agree on, but that somewhere along that road is a local guide who knows a story that we have never heard before, a story that leads to a place in the desert . . . where there is plenty of food and water.'[9]

---

7. Turner, *The Australian Dream*, 102.
8. Bill Neidjie, *Story About Feeling*, edited by Keith Taylor (Broome: Magabala Books, 1989), 3.
9. Stephen Muecke, *No Road (bitumen all the way)* (Fremantle WA: Fremantle Arts Centre Press, 1997), 130.

Change and Distance:
Unfished Business in Australia

Wounded we cross the desert's emptiness,
and must be false to what would make us whole.
For only change and distance shape for us
some new tremendous symbol of the soul.
                    (Judith Wright, 'The Harp And The King')

****

The question of relations between non-indigenous and indigenous peoples is becoming an increasingly urgent one, perhaps especially so in Australia where our leaders seem increasingly able to deal with it.[1] Yet it seems to me that the question is essentially an imaginative one. It is not just a matter, as some seem to think, of structural accommodation but of a profound cultural gap which needs to be bridged. In this task I believe that literature has an important part to play. So I would like to look at a recent novel, Kate Grenville's *The Secret River,*[2] to see what it has to offer.

Set in the early days of settlement, it is about one William Thornhill, transported to New South Wales from the slums of London in 1806 'for the term of his natural life' for stealing. Granted a ticket-of-leave, he takes up land on the banks of the Hawkesbury River and ends his life as a rich man. But he novel's central concern is with relations between the new settlers, the land and its Aboriginal inhabitants. To the extent that it is loosely based on the story of one of Grenville's

---

1. I owe this insight and many more to an unpublished doctoral thesis, 'Indigenous Peoples: Towards an Interconnective and Conscientising Dialogue' by Z Kutena, University of Western Sydney, 2005.
2. Kate Grenville, *The Secret River* (Melbourne: Text Publishing, 2005). All page reference will be given in the body of my text.

ancestors, it also can be seen as an interrogation of both personal
and national identity As Kerryn Goldsworthy remarks in her review
of the novel, 'one way of confronting the present is to interrogate the
past'.[3]

In many respects Thornhill is the typical 'pioneering hero' of
colonial myth, carving out a new life for himself and his family 'out
of a remote and monstrously difficult wilderness.'[4] But as Grenville
presents him, he is also a figure of some pathos since his life in the
slums of the East End has not equipped him to deal with the 'change
and distance', confronting him in this place so different from anything
he has known. The description of his first night in Sydney makes this
clear. Everything, even the night sky, is unfamiliar. 'There was no Pole
Star, a friend to guide him . . . No Bear that he had known all his life:
only this blaze, unreadable, indifferent', while around him stretches
'the vast fact pressing in, like 'some great sighing lung' breathing
around him.(5) This is the sense of displacement described in many
colonial novels, of feeling 'alone and friendless in the world' as '*The
Recollections Of Geoffrey Hamlyn* puts it, like a child in the dark'.[5]

He could feel the night, huge and damp, flowing in [through the
door of his makeshift hut] and bringing in with it the sounds of its
own life: tickings and creakings, small private rustlings, and beyond
that the soughing of the forest, mile after mile (3).

These feelings, of course, give the lie to the legal justification of
settlement, that this is *terra nullius,* an empty stage on which to play
out a scenario of power and prosperity. So, too, does the presence of its
indigenous inhabitants which confronts him even on this first night
as, stepping outside the hut in which he and his family have found
shelter, the darkness seems to move before him, 'a human, as black
as the night itself', wearing 'his nakedness like a cloak' and holding a
spear which seemed to be part of him. But the figure seems to have
a troubling dignity about him that interrogates Thornhill's sense of
his own humanity, making him, clothed as he was, feel 'skinless as
a maggot.' Without the resources to deal with this challenge, he can
only respond negatively, reacting in the only way he knows, with

---

3. Kerryn Godsworthy, 'A Room Made Of Leaves And Air', in *Australian Book
   Review,* 273 (August 2005): 10.
4. Ian Turner, editor, *The Australian Dream* (Melbourne: Sun Books, 1968), x.
5. JDS Mellick, *Portable Australian Authors: Henry Kingsley* (St Lucia, QLD:
   University of Queensland Press, 1982), 135.

violence: 'After so long as a felon, hunched under the threat of the lash, he felt himself expanding back into his full size' as he shouts '*Damn your eyes be off... Go to the devil!*' (5).

As Hayden White points out, this kind of self-definition by negation is especially useful for those 'whose dissatisfactions are easier to recognize than their programs are to justify'[6] In England Thornhill had been a nobody. But here he defines himself over against this other, as 'civilised' and the others as a 'savage', a lower form of life.[7] This process in in most of his fellow settlers, especially in the brutal and ignorant ex-convict 'Smasher' Sullivan, for whom the Aborigines whose land he had taken 'were nothing but thieving black buggers . . . taking advantage of a man's hard work' whom he was intent on 'learning a lesson whenever he saw them lurking about' (193). For his part Thornhill is content to defuse the threat their difference poses to his own sense of identity by denigration, giving the Aborigines he meets insulting names like 'Whisker Harry'—a habit common on the frontier, of course.

The result was that instead of being a place where different peoples met and came to understand one another, the frontier became a place of mutual incomprehension and violence. The official story of settlement, however, has played down this violence—our present Australian Prime Minister, for instance, has condemned what he calls the 'Black Armband School of History', the attempt to record what happened on the other side of the frontier to Aboriginal Australians. But Grenville is interested in understanding the sources of the division and conflict and avoiding Manichean divisions between good and evil, black and white, making her protagonist, William Thornhill, a 'man of quick temper and strong feeling', as the blurb describes him, an ambiguous figure.

In effect he emerges as the product of history, the history of empire on to which, according to Karl Jaspers, the West has 'loaded . . . a grandeur stolen from God',[8] believing ourselves the spearhead of civilization destined to rule the world, a rule to which all others, 'lesser breeds without the law', were to submit. True, until he reached

---

6. Hayden White, *Tropics of Discourse: Essays In Cultural Criticism* (London: John Hopkins University Press, 1978), 152.

7. White, *Tropics Of Discourse,* 170.

8. Lotte Kohler and Hans Saner, editors, *Correspondence Hannah Arendt Karl Jaspers* (New York: Harcourt Brace Book, 1992), 149.

New South Wales, Thornhill had been in many respects a victim of this system, a poor man transported for stealing, offending against property, the cornerstone of empire. But when in the new land he also acquires property he becomes an agent of empire, of Governor Macquarie's policy of granting convicts a ticket-of-leave so that they would take up land and expand settlement and thus guarantee the survival of the colony, helping to establish a 'new Britannia in another world'.[9]

Thornhill joins in enthusiastically. From his first glimpse of the plot of land on which he eventually settles he longs to possess it. In England the most someone like him might own was a few sticks of furniture, a few clothes and the tools of his trade. But land here was for the taking and he is even able to impose his name on it, and his passion for possession is almost religious in intensity. 'He had heard preachers mouthing about the Promised Land. He had taken it for another thing in the world that was just for the gentry. Nothing had ever been promised to him.' But here he is in charge. The land he covets is not 'promised . . . by God, but by himself, to himself.' (108)

He is thus the typical 'historical man', 'the man who *is* insofar as he *makes himself, within history*'[10] since he and his desires are his centre of value. According to Luiz Carlos Susin, who describes the authority, creates a self which distinguishes and identifies 'good and evil in a very particular way based on itself, on its glorious position as basis and referent of the whole of reality spread out at its feet.'[11] In this triumphal march, however, he comes in conflict with 'archaic man', the Aboriginal people whose feel themselves part of and bound not to history but 'indissolubly connected with the Cosmos and the cosmic rhythms'.[12] Confined within his 'closed circle around sameness',[13] however, Thornhill is unable to understand and deal with this culture.

Convinced of his superiority as a white man, he makes no attempt to understand or sympathise with the people he has dispossessed or to learn their language, and when he does attempt to communicate— significantly, to order them off the land he now regards as 'his'—

---

9. Turner, *The Australian Dream*, 10.
10. Mircea Eliade, *The Myth Of The Eternal Return Or, Cosmos And History* (Princeton: Princeton University Press, 1974), ix.
11. Luiz Carlos Susin, 'A Critique Of The Identity Paradigm', in *Concilium*, 2 (2000): 80.
12. Eliade, *The Myth Of The Eternal Return Or, Cosmos And History*, xiii.
13. Susin, 'A Critique Of The Identity Paradigm', 87.

the result is the mutual incomprehension which ultimately leads to the massacre in which he is more or less unwillingly involved. Yet his incomprehension is a determined one. When he discovers, for instance, that one of his sons has been spending time at the Aboriginal camp and is learning their language and skills, he flogs him: no son of his should share the ways of 'savages'. 'Civilisation' can only be preserved by doing away with what they represent.[14]

But the novel suggests that his underlying motive is fear, not just of their culture but of the land also to which they belong so intimately but which he finds menacing as a power he does not understand and is struggling to dominate. Sensing the unseen presence of the Aborigines watching him and his family, '[h]is hundred acres no longer felt quite his own' as 'their bodies flickered among the trees, as if the darkness of the men were an extension of bark, of leaf shade, of the play of light on a water-stained rock' (198). For him the land is to be brought under his control and made to serve his purposes whereas they serve its purposes.

Nonetheless the novel does not accept this division as the only one possible. Several of her characters have some feeling for and sympathy with the Aborigines and their culture, suggesting that the boundaries between the two cultures are not absolute and that we may have something to learn from them. Thomas Blackwood who first introduced Thornhill to the

Hawkesbury is one of them, settling down with an Aboriginal wife and child. He learns their language and becomes part of their community—to the disgust of his fellow settlers. Theirs is a culture of violence, of the 'war of every man against everyman' Thomas Hobbes described and which he attributed to the lack of 'a common power to keep them in awe'.[15] But Blackwood accepting and accommodating himself to the authority of the place and its people is prepared to 'take a little and give a little' (169). So too is Mrs Herring, perhaps because she is a widow and vulnerable but also because she is repulsed by the brutality of settlers like 'Smasher' Sullivan. Similarly, Thornhill's long-suffering wife Sal comes to see the Aborigines as fellow human beings when, homesick for England and lonely for the company of other

---

14. White, *Tropics Of Discourse: Essays In Cultural Criticism,* 154.
15. Thomas Hobbes, *Leviathan,* in MH Abrams *et al,* editors, *The Norton Anthology Of English Literature,* I, (New York: WW Norton, 1962), 1086.

women, she visits their camp and exchanges gifts with them, and these meetings continue. Later when the men come from the camp to ask the Thornhills to leave, realizing that her husband's instinct is to turn his gun on them, she shouts to him to offer them some food instead. Significantly for our purposes, there is a distinction being made here between what Helene Cixous calls the 'feminine', the 'economy of the gift' which is open to the other and ready to give to and receive from it and the 'masculine' economy which is preoccupied with property, propriety and appropriation and exerts control by violent means and repressing or destroying difference. The 'feminine' is ready to move across boundaries, since her centre of gravity is within the self where, as Cixous puts it, she 'has never ceased to hear the resonance of fore-language'.[16] Authority here is a matter of resonance, of listening, rather of the force on which the settlers rely. The distinction the novel makes here, I think, implicitly suggests that this is the way to the solution to the problem it is concerned with—and it is important that according to Cixous the distinction is not a matter of biology but of culture and indeed of imaginative flexibility.

Thornhill is a key figure in this respect since for a time he is beginning to hear this 'fore-language', to be aware of the 'archaic consciousness' of Aboriginal culture which gives them their affinity with the natural world. This begins when he visits the Aboriginal camp to demand that they leave what he now sees as 'his' land, with the implicit threat that they had 'best stay away out of it' (194). Yet despite himself he is impressed by the order, cleanliness and industry which confronts him there: the space is 'as clean-swept as the one around their own hut' and the two old women he sees by the fire, 'as still and dark as the ground they seemed to grow out of', (193) are hard at work rolling threads of stringybark into string. Somehow, too, their indifference to him and the authority he represents troubles him as they glance up at him 'with as little interest as if he were a fly come to watch them', as something seems to be telling him that this 'subaltern' culture might have an authority of its own.

When suddenly the men appear, 'arriving so quietly that they might have risen up out of the ground' (195), this feeling grows. Flustered, however, he tries to exert his authority, hailing them

---

16. Toril Moi, *Sexual/Textual Politics: Feminist Literary Criticism* (London: Routledge, 1991), 111–113.

jovially like a landlord welcoming tenants. But the words seem to 'evaporate', thin and silly into the air' as the old man he calls 'Whisker Harry' advances, radiating 'authority like heat off a fire', to place 'a long black hand on his forearm', ordering him and his family to leave. Neither side comprehends what the other is saying, and the move underlines the mutual incomprehension—an important point if we are to understand rather than demonise the clash between cultures.

> A conversation had taken place. There had been an inquiry
> and an answer.
> But what inquiry, which answer?
> They stared at each other, the words between them like a wall
> (197).

But Thornhill gradually retreats behind the wall of his culture as the Aborigines step up their attacks on the settlers in an attempt to drive them away. He has so much invested in the system to which he belongs that his ability to question it is limited. So when a clumsy military operation against them fails, he becomes increasingly embroiled with the settlers led by 'Smasher' Sullivan who are determined to take the law into their own hands. Feeling as if he 'had stepped on a great wheel that was spinning him away somewhere he had never planned to go', Thornhill nevertheless refuses to contemplate 'what that might mean, or where it might lead' (234). All he that he knows is that the first piece of property he has ever owned is threatened and must be defended.

This image of the machine reminds me of Heinrich Blucher's description of history as he contemplates the ruins of Europe after World War II as a 'social maelstrom which has smashed into [the world] . . . sweeping people along on its random undercurrent . . . driven by interests, that sucks us down into the depths'.[17] Though Thornhill is basically decent his interests, his newly acquired prosperity and the power that goes with it are drawing him into the violence planned by Sullivan and his allies. As the novel suggests in its account of his reaction when for the first time in his life he becomes a master of servants and bullies them as he himself had once been bullied, '[s]ome slow engine had been set in motion: wheels turning cogs meshing greasily' as he becomes part the culture of conquest and

---

17. Kohler and Saner, *Correspondence Hannah Arendt Karl Jaspers*, 149.

domination. 'New South Wales had a life of its own now, beyond any intention that any man—the Governor or even the King himself—might have. It was a machine in which some men would be crushed up and spat out, and others would rise to heights they would not have dreamed of before' (181–182).

Its values are pragmatic: as Blucher says it is the product of 'men who have lost sight of eternity'[18] So to preserve his interests Thornhill goes with the mob and joins in the massacre which leaves the settlers in sole possession of the area and finally makes him a rich man and master of a large estate and a grand house. But the closing scene in which he sits on his veranda 'where he could overlook all his wealth and take his ease' is an equivocal one. He cannot understand 'why his success did not feel like triumph'. But the novelist, it seems, can. Memories of the violence trouble him. 'The one thing that brought him a measure of peace' is to look to the cliffs on the other side of the river as darkness comes on, 'still blazing gold . . . glowing secretively with an after-light that seemed to come from inside the rocks themselves' (334).

It is not difficult to decipher what is being suggested since it recalls a long tradition in Australian writing, that there is some important secret in the land itself, 'some new tremendous symbol of the soul'. Judith Wright calls it, which it is our task as newcomers to discover, 'glowing secretly' beyond the limits of imperial history. By and large that history has seen the goal as economic development, the goal Thornhill achieved. But the novel's conclusion suggests rather that the primary task of settlement is, as Mircea Eliade puts it, imaginative, the task our writers, artists and musicians have been engaged in, the 'transformation of chaos into cosmos'.[19]

The novel suggests that one way of achieving this is to learn from the culture which has achieved this transformation, the culture of indigenous Australians. From time to time Thornhill has caught a glimpse this possibility, most clearly in the scene in which he witnesses a corroboree, the men dancing 'with their eyes full of light from the fire, the lines of white on their bodies twisting with life' and the women and children accompanying them on clapsticks and realises that he is in the presence of something sacred, a celebration of life itself, the life of the cosmos and of its authority.

---

18. Kohler and Saner, *Correspondence Hannah Arendt Karl Jaspers*, 149.
19. Eliade, *The Myth Of The Eternal Return Or*, 10.

The feet of the old man leading the dance 'seemed the pulse of the earth itself and when he began to sing, he threw the song up into the air, its long-crooked line the sound of the blood in the veins of the place itself' (244). Drawn despite himself into the sound, 'the beat of the sticks like the pumping of his own heart' (245), he is in the presence of another kind of authority, the authority of people who live in tune with the world as he, intent on using it for his own ends, will never be. He feels as he did when he, an illiterate, stood in the Governor's library awed by the 'rows of gleaming books with their gold lettering' which would reveal their secrets only to a person who knew how to read them. The old man leading the dance is a book and his people 'are reading him' (244). These people are where they belong, 'singing up the land' in a space imbued with spirit. The possibility of finding this space, I suggest, is 'glowing secretly in the after-life of our non-indigenous culture today.

The Secret River, then, has an important contribution to make to the problem of the troubled relations between indigenous and non-indigenous peoples, not only in Australia but elsewhere in the world, suggesting as it does, with Mircea Eliade, that the time may have come when, to ensure our survival we may have to desist from any further '"making" of history in the sense in which [we have been making it] from the creation of the first empires' and learn from cultures we have come to despise as 'primitive' to rediscover our place in the cosmos.[20]

---

20. Eliade, *The Myth Of The Eternal Return Or*, 153.

The Poetry Of Judith Wright And Ways Of Rejoicing In The World

Poetry, as WH Auden famously said, 'makes nothing happen'. But, he also said that . . . it survives.

In the valley of its saying where executives would never want to tamper since its great task is to 'persuade us to rejoice',[1] that is, to put us in touch with deeper sources of meaning by ridding us of a purely instrumental sense of the world in general and of place in particular in order to respond to the deeper possibilities it presents. According to Mircea Eliade it is a particularly urgent task for people in settler societies who find themselves in unfamiliar territory to make this transformation, from chaos into 'cosmos' and learn to live according to its rhythms.[2]

But this is not the way most settlers saw—or indeed still see. For them space was an empty container to be filled with sheep, cattle and crops, towns and cities or to be mined for minerals, an empty stage on which 'Nature's painted curtains are drawn aside to reveal heroic man at his epic labour on the stage of history'.[3] But growing problems, terrors even with which imperial history confronts us suggest that we may need, as Eliade said, to leave off from any further 'making' of this kind of history, redefine our notions of place and time to situate ourselves in the universe as a whole.[4]

1. WH Auden, 'In Memory of W B Yeats', in MH Abrams *et al*, editors *Norton Anthology of English Literature* (New York: Norton, 1965), 1627.
2. Mircea Eliade, *The Myth of The Eternal Return Or, Chaos And Cosmos* (Princeton: Princeton University Press, 1974), 10.
3. Paul Carter, *The Road to Botany Bay: An Essay in Spatial History* (London: Faber & Faber, 1987), xv.
4. Eliade, *The Myth of The Eternal Return Or, Chaos and Cosmos*, 153.

This is something that many of our poets, along with other artists, have attempted to do from the beginnings of settlement. Judith Wright is one of them. In her view the land has 'presented herself as the most difficult of technical problems', in the sense that to its early settlers it seemed hostile, 'the outer equivalent of an inner reality . . . the reality of exile.' Her task as a writer, then, she believed was to 'be at peace' with it. But for that 'it must first be observed, understood, described and as it were absorbed.'[5] Significantly, she began this work at a crisis point in our history when the country was threatened with invasion and she felt, her 'own blood and bone', 'beloved and imperilled'.[6]

The first poem in her Collected Poems is about the collision she senses between the time of imperial history in which she sees . . . no end to the breaking—one smashed, another mocks from your enemy's eye . . . nothing but the tick of the clock and a world sucked dry and the time of the land and its 'song [which] all life is learning', as it

> . . . grows around us, before us, behind,
> there is sound in the silence; the dark is a tremor of light.
> It is the corn rising when winter is done.[7]

For the rest of her career she was to dedicate herself to this music, aware that [t]he language and culture I was brought up in . . . had nothing to do with the land my relatives had taken. It was wholly imported, a second skin that never fitted, no matter how we pulled and dragged it over the landscape that we lived in. Nor, of course, did we ourselves fit. That fact was growing more obvious as the land changed under our hand.[8] The task therefore, to draw on Heidegger's distinction, was to learn to dwell *in* rather than merely to build *on* the land.[9]

---

5. Judith Wright, *Preoccupations in Australian Poetry* (Melbourne: Oxford University Press, 1966), xi.
6. Veronica Brady, *South of My Days: A Biography Of Judith Wright* (Sydney: Angus & Robertson, 1998), 88.
7. Judith Wright, 'The Moving Image', in *Judith Wright: Collected Poems 1942-1985* (Sydney: Angus&Robertson, 1994), 3–6. Hereafter referred to as *CP*.
8. Brady, *South Of My Days*, 121.
9. Martin Heidegger, 'Building Dwelling Thinking', in *Poetry, Language, Thought* (New York, Harper Colophon Books, 1975), 143–162.

Her early poems, however, were about the New England tableland where she had grown up and where, for all that she identified with the land, feeling that '[t]he long slopes' concurrence is my flesh who am the gazer and the land I stare on there was also a sense of exile, ancestral memory as 'sullenly the jealous bones' recalled the 'other earth' that was also 'shaped and hoarded in them.' The colonial self wants to conquer and possess the land. Only then will my land turn sweetly from the plough and all my pastures rise green as spring. ('For New England', *CP*, 22–23)

To do that the first step was to let go the long commentary of the brain' ('Sonnet', *CP*, 16), the 'one-sided masculinity and narrowness of thought' which, she was coming to see, led 'nowhere but to a world scarcely worth living in that, clearly . . . was on a slide to its own destruction'.[10] This meant embracing a different kind of logic, the 'feminine', what Helene Cixous[11] calls the 'economy of the gift' which is open to the other, giving and receiving, and lives from within, listening, as another poem has it, for and to 'the word, that, when all words are said, / shall compass more than speech.' ('Sonnet', *CP*, 16)

Wright's experience of motherhood drew her into this economy. In 'Woman To Child', for instance, the self becomes one with the ongoing creative process of the cosmos:

> Then all a world I made in me;
> all the world you hear and see
> hung upon my dreaming blood
>
> There moved the multitudinous stars,
> and coloured birds and fishes moved.
> There swam the sliding continents.
>
> ('Woman To Child', *CP*, 28)

Poetry thus became what Heidegger called 'the topology of Being' since it . . . tells Being the whereabouts of its actual presence,[12] moving it beyond 'the private archaeology of a subject' to become part of 'the

---

10. Brady, *South Of My Days*, 121.
11. Brady, *South Of My Days*, 121.
12. Toril Moi, *Sexual/Textual Politics: Feminist Literary Theory* (London: Routledge, 1991), 111–113.

folklore for humanity as a whole',[13] challenging the separation of the physical and the psychic which is characteristic of Western culture today, which, to refer to Cixous again, is essentially 'masculine', living according to the 'economy of the proper, preoccupied with property, propriety and appropriation.[14]

Romantic as this may seem, it nevertheless echoes current scientific thinking which sees the physical universe as more open, subtle and supple than has been thought, regards humanity's place in it as more problematic and tends to study relations rather than single objects.[15] Similarly in her poetry Wright was increasingly aware of actual living forces and interdependences at work in the world and of human beings as 'part of this wider process and subordinate to its laws',[16] rejoicing in it, however, rather than deploring it:

> . . . [W]ho wants to be a mere onlooker? Every cell of me
> has been pierced through by plunging intergalactic messages.
> ('Connections', *CP*, 422)

Poetry of this kind has little to do with mere self-expression. Its task rather, as Rilke said, is to name the world, but 'with an intensity the things themselves never / hoped to achieve',[17] recognising in them a power beyond the self which is often awesome and sometimes terrible but demands expression:

> . . . The voice is not our own
> and yet its tone's deeper than intimate,
> comes from elsewhere and compels obedience.

> . . . [W]hen, expected and entreated long,
> the question comes, we cannot hesitate,
> but, turning blindly, put all else away.
> ('Poem And Audience', *CP*, 210)

---

13. Martin Heidegger, 'The Thinker as Poet', in *Poetry, Language, Thought* (New York: Harper, 1975).
14. Moi, *Sexual/Textual Politics*, 111.
15. Paul Ricoeur, *The Symbolism of Evil* (Boston: Beacon Press, 1969), 12.
16. Brady, *South of My Days*, 287.
17. Brady, *South of My Days*, 266.

That, I suggest, is why in Wright's poetry, her nature poetry especially, one often senses a certain bafflement, a feeling of being overpowered by what it is attempting to depict. 'Nameless Flower', for instance, opens with a fairly confident description of

> Three white petals float
> above the green,
> asserting that
> I'll set a word upon a word
> to be your home.

But self-confidence diminishes as wonder increases, and the poem concludes with something like defeat:

> Word and word are chosen and met.
> Flower, come in.
> But before the trap is set,
> the prey is gone.
>
> The words are white as a stone is white
> carved for a grave;
> but the flower blooms in immortal light,
> Being now; being love.
>
> ('Nameless Flower', *CP,* 130.)

The encounter here is peaceful enough. But other poems are not. In 'Dust', written in the midst of drought, the 'sick dust, spiralling with the wind' is accusatory:

> . . . our dream was the wrong dream,
> our strength was the wrong strength.
> Weary as we are we must make a new choice.
>
> (*CP,* 23–24)

As the devastation of the environment became more apparent, it is the poet herself who identifies with the land to make the accusation. 'At A Public Dinner', for example, presents 'developers' as cannibals:

> No, I'm not eating. I'll watch the champing jaws,
> solemnly eating and drinking my country's honour,
> my country's flesh. The gravy's dripping red,
> a nourishing stew for business. She's a goner.
>
> (*CP,* 312)

'Jet Flight Over Derby', describing flight over eroded country in the north-west, 'worn red lands', continues this indictment. Yet it is to them, not to the 'bird-tracked air' in which she is merely a 'travelling eye' that she commits herself. Her body

> ... knows its place
> and longs to stand on land,
> ... I am what land has made
> And land's myself, I said.

She has known this from childhood—'Most children are brought up in the 'I' tradition—the ego, it's me and what I think. But when you live in very close contact with a large and splendid landscape you feel yourself a good deal smaller than just I',[18] and she refuses to back-away from this commitment:

> And therefore, when land dies?
> opened by whips of greed
> these plains lie torn and scarred.
> Then I erode; my blood
> Reddens the stream in flood.
>   ('Jet Flight Over Derby', *CP,* 279–280)

Here she has much in common with Aboriginal people. As one of their leaders Patrick Dodson observes, 'many Australians don't know how to think themselves into country, into the world. We Aboriginal people find it hard to think without the land.'[19] Another angry poem written about the same time 'Australia 1970' which opens with the angry apostrophe,

> Die, wild country, like the eagle hawk,
> dangerous till the last breath's gone,
> clawing and striking
>
>   (*CP,* 287)

further echoes the sense of the land as a living power, expressed by two Aboriginal women from the north-west: 'Country knows who

---

18. Brady, *South Of My Days,* 469.
19. Kevin Keeffe *Paddy's Road: Life Stories of Patrick Dodson* (Canberra: Aboriginal Studies Press, 2003), 35.

is walking about in it. It can feel who is there. It knows if a stranger comes, and it can get angry. Start a bushfire or something.'[20]

At the same time Wright was aware that she came 'of a conquering people' and was one of the 'invaders'. But precisely because 'no land is lost or won by wars, / for earth is spirit' ('At Cooloola', *CP,* 140), she sensed an unpaid debt to the land's First Peoples. As 'Nigger's Leap, New England', a meditation on a nineteenth century massacre, put it, it was

> . . . their blood channelled our rivers,
> and the black dust our crops ate was their dust.
> > ('Nigger's Leap, New England, *CP,* 15)

But over time, as she made Aboriginal friends, especially with the poet and activist Oodgeroo Noonuccal (Kath Walker), a common grief for the land drew them together. As she wrote to Oodgeroo:

> If we are sisters, it's in this—
> our grief for a lost country,
> the place we dreamed in long ago,
> poisoned now and crumbling.
> > ('Two Dreamtimes', *CP,* 316)

She also came to realise that in wounding the land and its First Peoples we had also wounded ourselves so that

> [s]omething leaks in our blood
> like the ooze from a wound,

speaking from

> a depth that rhymes our pride
> with its alternative.
> > ('The Dark Ones', *CP,* 354–345)

To conclude then. Judith Wright's poetry becomes a point of entry into the life of the cosmos away from the chaos of contemporary history.

---

20. Catherine Landine, 'Sentient Country, Deferential People', in John Cameron, editor, *Changing Places: Reimagining Australia* (Sydney: Longueville Books, 2003), 6.

It also challenges the complacent belief that human consciousness is the absolute centre of existence, suggesting rather that, Levinas has it, 'it is . . . in the laying down by the ego of its sovereignty . . . that we find ethics and also probably the very spirituality of the soul, but most certainly the question of the meaning of being.'[21] That meaning exceeds our understanding and control. But it is to be affirmed and celebrated—as one of Wright's last poems insists:

> I hang on the rockpool's edge, its wild embroideries;
> admire it, pore on it, this, the devouring and mating,
> ridges of coloured tracery, occupants, all the living.
> the stretching of toothed claws to food, the breeding
> on the ocean's edge. 'Accept it? Gad, madam, you had better.'[22]
>
> (*CP*, 419)

If it is true, as Auden said, that 'poetry makes nothing happen', it may nevertheless 'persuade us to rejoice' even in the dangerous times in which we live. Wright's poetry makes what she calls the 'size and silence'[23] of Australia and its painful recent history a gift to our times, reminding us that, to quote Levinas again, it may be necessary 'to prefer that which justifies being than that which assures it.'[24]

---

21. Sean Hand, editor, *The Levinas Reader* (Oxford: Wiley-Blackwell, 1993), 85.
22. The quotation is Samuel Johnson's reply to a rather silly woman who said to him that 'on the whole I accept life.'
23. *Preoccupations In Australian Poetry*, xii.
24. Hand, *The Levinas Reader*, 85.

Called By The Land Into The Land

Let me begin with Mircea Eliade's suggestion that it is not inadmissible to think of an epoch, and an epoch not too far distant, when humanity, to ensure its survival, will find itself reduced to desisting from any further 'making' of history in the sense in which it began to make it from the creation of the first empires, will confine itself to repeating archetypal gestures.[1] So far, we non-Aboriginal Australians, part of the expansion of Europe over recent centuries and only recently arrived in what Bernard O'Dowd called this 'Last sea-thing dredged by sailor Time from Space',[2] have barely be begun this task which calls on us not merely to *build* on the land, to exploit it for our own purposes and profit, but to learn to *dwell* in it,[3] live with it respectfully and intimately—as its First Peoples have done since time immemorial.

True, since our arrival we have devised myths, stories of explorers, 'Little Aussie Battlers', the Anzacs, sporting heroes and heroines, and so on. By and large, however, Aboriginal Australians have been absent from absent from this list—indeed their existence is not even mentioned in the Constitution, for example—of the imperial history which brought us here, concerning ourselves with events on our side of the frontier and seeing Aboriginal Australia as its negative, its shadow, what Jung called 'the sum of all those unpleasant qualities we like to hide, together with the insufficiently developed functions and the

---

1. Mircea Eliade, *The Myth of the Eternal Return or, Cosmos and History* (Princeton: Princeton University Press, 1974), 153–154.
2. Bernard O'Dowd, 'Australia', in HP Heseltine, editor, *The Penguin Book of Australian Verse* (Ringwood, Vic: Penguin, 1972), 190
3. Martin Heidegger, *Poetry, Language, Thought* (New York: Harper Colophon Books, 19761975), 90–143.

contents of the personal unconscious' so that, as he goes on to argue, it becomes 'a moral problem that challenges the whole ego-personality' and require 'considerable moral effort'[4] is required to confront it.

As Deborah Bird Rose says, since we arrived here for its First Peoples this land has become 'a place of invasion, death, betrayal, hardship and cruelty'.[5] But many, perhaps most, of us are not prepared to consider, much less accept, this—understandably since, as Jung pointed out, we are 'on the whole less good than [we] imagine [ourselves] or want to be' and therefore do not want to explore the shadow side of ourselves or of our history. But as he says, suppressing the shadow is 'as little remedy as a beheading would be for a head ache: the more we ignore it, 'the 'the blacker and denser' it tends to become.[6]

Judith Wright's 'Shadow', the concluding poem of her *Collected Poems*,[7] however, attempts to confront the problem, set on the edge of a cliff at nightfall as darkness wells up from the valley below rising 'upward silently' to announce 'that it was I', come 'to master me' with the power of

> ... negating night
> that counterpoints the day
> and deepens into fear
> of time that falls away,
> of self that vanishes
> till eyes stare outward blind
> on one invading darkness
> that brims from earth to mind.

But this confrontation is not entirely negative since it is a reminder that as human beings we are part of the larger life of the universe. This is the subject of several poems published in the 1960s. 'The Lake' (192) is perhaps the most explicit. Seen as the 'eye of the earth', its 'candid staring' interrogates her complacent assumption that 'my meaning's what you are', suggesting that our task is to respect the world in which we live

---

4. Carl Jung, *Jung Selected Writings*, introduced by Anthony Storr (London: A Fontana Original, 1986), 91.
5. Deborah Bird Rose, *Reports From a Wild Country* (Sydney: University of New South Wales Press, 2004), 3.
6. Carl Jung, *Jung*, 88.
7. Judith Wright, *Collected Poems 1942–1985* (Sydney: Angus & Robertson, 1994). Hereafter page references are to poems discussed and will be given in the text of the essay.

You see no tree nor cloud. That's what I take
out of your waters in this net I cast—
the net where time is knotted by the word,
that flying needle

and learn from and attempt to name its beauty and its terror:

sun, moon and cloud, the hanging leaves and trees,
and leaning through, the terrible face of man;
my face

and beyond that to move to a more profound encounter which cannot
be named but only experienced:

. . . I looked, and there my eyes met eyes,
Lover to lover. Deep I looked, and saw.

The poem which follows this, 'Interplay', points away from the self
into cosmic space:

Look how the stars' bright chaos eddies in
to form our constellations. Flame by flame
answers the ordering image in the name.
World's signed with words: there light—there love begin.

This brings us back to the challenge of Aboriginal Australia and the
need to confront it, so that as Patrick White put it we may become
a 'people possessed of understanding', aware of the full range of the
'privilege and panic' of our humanity, in particular of its 'terrible
face' which the imperial self has tended to ignore and a reflection of
the 'privilege and panic' of humanity in a world 'signed with words'
where 'light [and] . . . love begin panic'[8] of existence as a whole:

sun, moon and cloud the hanging leaves and trees,
and leaning through the terrible face of man.

To a greater or lesser extent, I suspect that fear of this kind of negation
has haunted us as a people ever since our arrival in this unfamiliar

---

8. This, of course, is the implicit theme of his novel *Voss* and he puts it explicitly in
his memoir *Flaws in the Glass* (London: Cape, 1980), 104 in which he describes
us as 'child-adults' who 'shy away from the deep end of the unconscious'.

land on the other side of the world from those from which we came and has also increased our anxiety in the presence of its First Peoples who have lived with it so long and so intimately whose lives and culture have been profoundly disrupted and damaged by our arrival.

Another of Wright's poems, 'The Dark Ones', explores this anxiety. It is set in a typical country town on pension day when the Aboriginal fringe dwellers, normally invisible, 'the dark ones',

> [t]he night ghosts of a land
> only by day possessed,

appear in town. The 'night ghosts of the self, 'the "negative" aspect of the personality, the sum of all those unpleasant qualities we like to hide, together with the insufficiently developed functions and the contents of the personal unconscious,'9 and only in that way can 'chaos' be contained. This, of course, is the point Jung makes. But I want to argue that this could be said of Australian culture today, that we need to come to terms with its shadow side, Aboriginal Australia as Bird Rose describes it since, as she goes on to say, as well as being a place of suffering and humiliation it is also the place of 'resilience, survival, story-telling and unswerving belief that things could be different'.10 'Different' are also to be found there. The problem then arises how to enter into a relationship which is mutually respectful.

An incident one night at a recent conference has become a kind of parable for me. of parable for me. One of our keynote speakers, an Aboriginal man, returned late one night to find himself locked out of the college in which the rest of us were staying and were already asleep and was unable to wake anyone to let him in. So, scouting around, he found two large rubbish bins, then piled one on top of the other, climbed on top and from there was able to reach the balcony to his room and pull himself in. For me this has become an image of their present situation outsiders in the land in which their ancestors lived from time immemorial and a reminder that we and they occupy the same land, though in reality we, not they, who are the intruders and that they have claims to make on us and possess skills and understandings which we do not and may therefore have a great deal to teach us about the land but also about ourselves.

---

9. Judith Wright, *CP,* 29872988.
10. Bird Rose, Reports, 4.

What has happened to them since our arrival, for instance, suggests that we may not be the people our official national anthem 'Advance Australia Fair' proclaims us to be, 'young and free', advancing confidently across 'boundless plains' into a future of material abundance and that in reality our unofficial anthem 'Waltzing Matilda' may have more important things to tell us about ourselves, concluding as it does with the swagman's leap into the billabong, which I see metaphorically as a descent into the unacknowledged depths of the self and of the shadow side of our history, the story of Aboriginal Australia and its peoples.

To enter into it imaginatively, however, may be more demanding than we think—as another of Judith Wright's poems, 'The Dark Ones', suggests. It is set unromantically in a typical country town on pension day when the Aboriginal fringe dwellers appear in town to collect their money. As Wright sees them, they are

> [t]he night ghosts of a land
> only by day possessed
> who come haunting into the mind
> like a shadow cast,

reminding us of what we do not want to know, that our

> [d]ay has another side.
> Night has its time to live,
> a depth that rhymes our pride
> with its alternative.[11]

Personally I sensed something like this from time to time as a child when we were exploring the bush outside the country town in which we were living at the time. I sensed this myself from time to time as a child in the bush, feeling a presence there which did not like me and now I realise that this may have been the presence of 'the Suffering Servant' of Isaiah's prophecy, 'wounded for our iniquities and bruised for our sins'.

But the Suffering Servant was to bring new life and I suggest that Aboriginal Australia may have this to offer us also. By and large, our present culture rests on the separation between self and world implicit in Descartes' proposition, 'I think. Therefore I am.' But as Kakadu elder Bill Neidjie expresses it, their relationship with the world is much more intimate:

11. 'The Dark Ones,' Wright, *CP*, 354.

> . . . Earth just like mother
> And father and brother of you.
> That tree same thing.
> Your body, my body I suppose,
> I'm same as you . . . anyone.
> Tree working when you sleeping or dream.

The relationship is respectful, even loving,

> feeling with my blood or body
> feeling all this tree and country

in a mutual relationship:

> While you sitting down e blow,
> You feel it wind
> And same this country you can look
> But feeling make you.[12]

This world-view looks beyond the self and beyond history to the great community of existence—a move surely necessary in the times in which we live if we are to cope with the environmental and personal challenges we face. But it is in this land, one of the most ancient but also politically one of the newest, we are still to find our place in the cosmic scheme which would enable us to belong properly. But there is no reason apart from our own unwillingness and lack of imagination why we should not achieve this and so respond to what Judith Wright called 'the word that, when all words are said, shall compass more than speech,'[13] the word of the land which Aboriginal Australia has been listening to for so long.

So let me leave you with the question Wright posed in one of her essays: 'will our lives or do we work out some inescapable inner logic?'[14]—a logic calling us to look beyond history and repeat the archetypal gestures which express 'knowledge of levels of reality otherwise inaccessible' to us.

---

12. Bill Neidjie, *Story About Feeling*, edited by Keith Taylor (Broome: Magabala Books, 1989), 3.
13. 'Sonnet', in Wright, *CP*, 16.
14. Judith Wright, *Because I Was Invited* (Melbourne: Oxford University Press, 1975), 85.

Human Distress And Suffering And The Question Of The Holocaust: Primo Levi's *If This Is A Man*

Literature, being what it is, has an abiding concern with human suffering, not because it is a good thing but because it is not, should not be and is an offence against our notions of justice. True, destruction as well as creation is the law of life as a whole. But what we hope is that in the long run creation will prevail. This is a truth which literature attempts to explore. There is no time here to explore the range of works of this kind. Instead let us focus on one work, Primo Levi's account of his sufferings as a prisoner in Auschwitz, *Se Queso E Un Uomo*, (*If This Is A Man*), a work which he wrote, he said, to liberate himself at last from his memories by staring them down and confronting the questions they pose.[1] True, in fact in the long run perhaps he did not succeed, since years later, still haunted he committed suicide. Nevertheless, the record he left of his struggle to survive remains profoundly illuminating.

It is also the stuff of tragedy, even if it is not written in tragic form. Certainly, the title, *If This Is A Man*, poses the essential tragic question: how human dignity can be sustained in the face of overwhelming suffering. In fact, the book is a record of courage, the determination not to give way before it. But it also suggests the way in which courage renders suffering less intolerable and endows it with tragic dignity as the individual appeals away from the disastrous present to a perspective beyond history in which a more expansive notion of justice may be found. In a time like ours, of course, this kind of appeal to an order beyond the self and its desires and understanding, the kind

---

1. I am using the French translation from the Italian, *Si C'est Un Homme* (Paris: Julliard, 1987). The translation is mine. All page references will be given in the text.

of understanding which is the stuff of classical tragedy and of works like the *The Book of Job* seems increasingly difficult to sustain. But that, I suggest, is the reason why what Levi has to say is so important.

The situation he describes—in which he and thousands of others found themselves in Nazi concentration camps—is the world Nietzsche described in his vision of a world in which God has ceased to exist. Allowances made for differences of scale, however, it also resembles the world in which today many people suffering in various ways find themselves, solitary and straying 'as through an infinite space . . . feeling the breath of [this] empty space' in which direction and meaning no longer have disappeared.[2] All that existed, it seemed, was subjected as they were to the brutalities of a system intent on their humiliation and destruction, pain, hunger, cold and exhaustion.

Without purpose or meaning each suffered alone without hope of release, trapped in a machine designed to exterminate them, forgotten by the rest of the world. Friends and country left behind, they existed beyond the pale of reason and decency in which 'there [was] no where' or even why' (34), ruled by a 'geometric madness' (64) which was determined to rob its victims of dignity and hope and reduce them to a 'stupor' (16) to which no alternative seemed possible (17) since it was a world without passion. As Levi recalled it, for example, even when the guards struck them they did so mechanically, showing no emotion. It was as if they were the victims of a 'wickedness beyond evil', of an ethical collapse which rendered their tormentors unable to comprehend what they were doing or take any responsibility for it.

The suffering of their victims was metaphysical as well as physical to the extent that this evil was their environment. This kind of suffering is what Simone Weil called 'affliction' a sense of being uprootedness, as if one is already dead to what is properly human and is filled with self-disgust at this condition.[3] The question implicit in the title of Levi's book, *If This Is A Man* suggests this kind of suffering. The fate of the people he describes, robbed of dignity, hope and any real power to resist it, lacks the splendour of tragedy since choice has nothing to do with their situation. A figure like Lear, for example, is in a sense responsible for his fate so that there is a certain justice in it since he had overstepped the limit, claiming limitless power for

2.   Simone Weil, *Waiting For God* (New York, Capricorn Books, 1959), 118.

3.   Walter Kaufmann, editor, *The Portable Nietzsche* (Ringwood: Penguin, 1968), 95.

himself and demanding absolute obedience to his desires. Levi and others, however, were overwhelmed by forces completely beyond their control and overwhelmed by the brutality, the 'venomous fruit' (262) of a system based on hatred and mindless fear, the *ressentiment* which Nietzsche saw as the revolt of slaves but which Levi believed is a 'latent infection' (7) in all of us.

What makes affliction of this kind so devastating is that goodness and justice no longer seem to exist, the world Nietzsche's madman described in which God is dead since we have murdered him and are now 'straying as through an infinite nothing.'[4] What is important about Levi's book, however, is that even here he manages to recover his dignity and even find hope in the midst of his suffering, glimpsing a kind of meaning in it. In our present context, I think, this matters because many, if not most people in affluent societies like ours are afflicted by apparent meaningless of their suffering or of the suffering of others.

Levi's revelation comes, significantly, from literature, from a discovery of a resource within our culture which enables him to draw new meaning from old definitions which no longer seem appropriate, a meaning directed to a goodness that transcends our current ability to understand what it is. The passage is from Dante's *Inferno* in which Dante meets Ulysses in the depths of hell who then tells him how he came to be here. In the freezing middle of winter as Levi and another prisoner on canteen duty were carrying the daily ration of soup through the snow from the kitchen to the hut in which their fellows were waiting this passage suddenly and inexplicably came into his mind. Ulysses begins with the exultant moment as he and his crew sailed through the Pillars of Hercules into the ocean and a new and unknown world opened out before them. This is for Levi a painful moment as he is moved by the distance between this moment of liberation and of new possibilities opening out before Ulysses and his crew and the situation which he and his fellow prisoners must endure and Ulysses' mention of the mountain they glimpsed inland as they sailed through the straits increases this pain since it reminds Levi of mountains he used to see in the distance when he was returning home as a free man.

---

4. An insight I owe to Charles Taylor, 'A Different Kind Of Courage', in *New York Review Of Books* (26 April, 2007): 6.

Ulysses' address to his crew at this moment seem at first to intensify the contrast:

> Brothers,' I said, 'o you, who having crossed
> a hundred thousand dangers, reach the west,
> to this brief waking time that still is left
>   unto your senses, you must not deny
> experience of that which lies beyond
> the sun, and of the world that is unpeopled.
>   Consider well the seed that gave you birth;
> You were not made to live your lives as brutes,
> But to be followers of worth and knowledge.[5]

But then as he reflects on them he seemed to be hearing these for the first time and it was as if they rang out 'like trumpets, like the voice of God' (149) reminding him in the midst of his exhaustion and despair of the resolve he had made when he first arrived at Auschwitz never to submit or inwardly accept the monstrous regime which had imprisoned him (65). The words 'you were not made to live your lives like brutes' reminded him of the belief he once had in his essential dignity as a human being. But Ulysses' exhortation to his men which follows was even more rousing, calling them to explore 'the world that is unpeopled' which 'lies beyond the sun' points to some vast imperishable world elsewhere which we are born to explore. This, he suddenly realised, applied to him also but to all who suffer.

Disastrous as it first appears, what happened next to Ulysses and his men extended this realisation:

> . . . [O]ut of that new land a whirlwind rose
> and hammered at our ship, against her bow.
>   Three times it turned her round with all the waters;
> and at the fourth, it lifted up the stern,
> so that our prow plunged deep, as pleased an Other,
>   until the sea again closed—over us.[6]

The phrase 'as pleased the Other' is the key since it suggests that there is a logic to Ulysses' fate since a larger order, some 'world which lies

---

5. *The Divine Comedy Of Dante Alighieri,* translated by Allen Mandelbaum (New York: Bantam Books, 1982), *Inferno,* XXVI, 112–118, 245.
6. *The Divine Comedy Of Dante Alighieri,* XXVI, 137–142, 244.

beyond the sun' perhaps in which it makes sense. This is the kind of insight Job also reaches at the end of his story when he bows down before 'things too wonderful for me, which I did not know'.[7] At this moment Levi who had been reciting the passage to his companion broke off, telling him that it was absolutely essential that he listen intently to the passage, that he must understand the significance of the phrase 'as pleased the Other' before it was too late. It might seem anachronistic, words from the long past Middle Ages but which nevertheless contained the explanation of their destiny and their presence here (151).

As Levi realised, few of us today in a desacralised culture believe in this 'Other' whose power and logic we must accept. For most of us the individual is seen as self-sufficient and more or less obliged to realise his/her desires wherever they may lead. But in this passage Dante implies that we human beings are part of cosmic order and owe obedience to its laws so that for him Ulysses' fate is understandable. He is being punished for sacrilege, for defying this order and asserting his desires against it and therefore bears some responsibility for his fate, giving it some meaning and dignity. According to Levi this incident enabled him to survive. Not that he could share Dante's belief, but he was able to glimpse the possibility of some order, a justice and goodness beyond history and beyond his understanding. As Charles Taylor says, faith in this order rather than in history demands courage. But it may be the best that is possible in the midst of suffering since it makes it possible to avoid despair.[8] This is not easy, of course. As Emmanuel Levinas puts it, 'modern man persists in his being as a sovereign who is . . . concerned to maintain the powers of his sovereignty',[9] believing that the world should serve his/her needs and demands. But the fate of Levi and thousands, possibly millions, like him in the world today, to say nothing of physical and mental suffering and death suggest that this is a destructive and dangerous illusion and that to sustain ourselves we must, to quote Charles Taylor again, we must attempt to live a life we do not understand and find some hope in looking beyond our present understanding.

---

7. *Job*, 42:3.
8. Taylor, 'A Different Kind Of Courage', 6.
9. Sean Hand, editor, *The Levinas Reader*. (Oxford: Wiley-Blackwell, 1993), 78.

In effect this is a view which could be called theological, since it involves the recognition of some mysterious authority beyond the self, the authority of existence itself. As we have said, this is not a fashionable position today; many indeed would see it as dishonest and even disreputable. It is significant, however, that in the 1930s in the midst of the Great Depression and the growing power of Nazism, Fascism and Stalinism thinkers like Walter Benjamin and later in the aftermath of World War II Hannah Arendt and Karl Jaspers seemed also to be making a similar response. Disillusioned with the direction in which contemporary history was moving—Heinrich Blucher, Arendt's partner, for instance, saw it as a 'societal maelstrom' which was creating 'a boiling mass of ghostlike, solitary individuals'[10]—they were echoing Nietzsche's denunciation of 'the "true world"' which, he believed, must be abolished and his call for a 'transvaluation of value.' Blucher was particularly scornful of the notion of 'progress', the preoccupation with the future which not only was prepared to sacrifice the present to its demands but also ignored the wisdom of the past, as if, he wrote, 'a future could ever open up for human beings who have lost sight of eternity'[11]—as Levi also came to suspect as he recalled Dante's insight.

But it is perhaps Walter Benjamin whose work is most relevant here. Like Levi he was Jewish and in its last phase could be seen as a response to Nazism—in fact he died on the border between France and Spain attempting to escape from it. He too was appalled by what he saw as the 'storm of history' driving towards the future, leaving behind it a pile of ruins.[12] The only hope he saw in it was theology, belief in the trans-historical reality Levi also glimpsed. Comparing it to a dwarf, 'small and ugly nowadays which cannot show itself under any circumstance', he nevertheless believed that ultimately it animates and manipulates the course of human affairs.[13] The reason for this belief brings us back to Levi since he saw the human lot as

---

10. Lotte Kohler and Hans Saner, editors, *Correspondence Hannah Arendt Karl Jaspers* (New York, Harcourt Brace Harvest Book, 1992), 278.

11. Kohler and Saner, *Correspondence Hannah Arendt Karl Jaspers,* 278.

12. Bram Mertens, '"Hope, Yes, But Not For Us": Messianism And Redemption In The Work Of Walter Benjamin', in Wayne Cristaudo and Wendy Baker, editors, *Messianism Apocalypse In 20th Century German Thought* (Adelaide: ATF Press, 2006), 73.

13. Mertens, '"Hope, Yes, But Not For Us"', 69.

a 'communion of suffering'—a view very different from the idea of history as 'progress'—usually defined in material terms.

For Benjamin therefore it was not the 'winners' but the losers who mattered since their fate had a meaning as yet unrealised which once understood would take the human story in a different direction. This meaning, he thought, would be only intelligible to theological categories since these categories alone, as his friend and colleague Theodor Adorno wrote, offered the hope of 'something that would differ from the unspeakable world that is'.[14] This, I would argue, is the kind of hope Levi glimpsed that winter's day in the midst of the apparent hopelessness of his situation—as his comment on the effect of his intuition then that an order exists beyond this one suggests.

It also suggests that, like Benjamin, he recognised a 'community of suffering'—a crucial matter in his situation where the feeling of isolation from the rest of humanity and of having to suffer alone was one of the worst of his sufferings. But he describes with something like awe, for instance, an incident one freezing night when one of his fellow prisoners got out of his bunk to care for another who was dying of dysentery and lying on the floor in his own mess to clean him, using his own ragged shirt to do so. The man may seem physically disgusting but this gesture recognises his dignity as a human being— kind of recognition, of course, which is the due of all those who suffer in any way. Other acts of kindness and concern, infrequent as they were, pointing beyond the 'unspeakable world' in which they were imprisoned, also sustained him.

According to Adorno such gestures expressed 'the only philosophy that can be responsibly practised in the face of despair . . . the attempt to contemplate all things as they would present themselves from the standpoint of redemption',[15] 'redemption' being seen here as a recognition of an abiding order elsewhere, the 'eternity' Blucher invoked against the history of 'progress' in whose perspective even a man dying in squalor demands respect and care. As Simone Weil would see it, this was a moment of the 'grace' which she sets over against the 'gravity' of brutal physical necessity, an illumination which penetrates to the centre of the self, illuminating its whole being

---

14. David Kaufmann, 'In The Light Of "The light Of Transcendence": Redemption In Adorno', in Wayne Cristaudo and Wendy Baker, editors, *Messianism, Apocalypse & Redemption In 20ᵗʰ Century German Thought* (Adelaide: ATF Press, 20060, 41.

15. Kaufmann, 'In The Light Of "The light Of Transcendence", 36.

and while conquering the brutal meaninglessness of suffering with the intuition that ultimately goodness and justice, incomprehensible as it may seem, still exists.[16] It is this kind of grace, I suggest, which comes to Lear in his last moments when Cordelia bends over him and he sees the love and forgiveness in her eyes, bringing with it a joy so powerful that it breaks his heart. It may be too much for him, but Adorno writes that the hope this grace brings, 'wrested from reality by negating it', is nevertheless the only form in which truth may appear in the midst of such extreme suffering.[17]

For Lear and other tragic figures like Othello and Oedipus it is true, grace comes too late and the distance between this truth and their situation proves unendurable. But for Levi, to return to him, the possibility of an order other than the brutal one intent on destroying him and the people to whom he belongs enables him to endure. In its light it seems as if his tormenters are not merely criminals but also fools who are not properly human (128). So it matters profoundly that he should bear his sufferings and if possible survive. But what of people suffering in less extreme situations, especially if their suffering is not, as his were, clearly the result of human malevolence? How is it possible for someone grieving the loss of a child or suffering from cancer, for instance, to believe in an ultimate order which is good and just?

Simone Weil has useful things to say about this problem. According to her 'the great enigma of human life is not suffering but affliction', a feeling of meaninglessness which 'stamps the soul to its very depths with the scorn, the disgust and even the self-hatred and sense of guilt and defilement that crime logically should produce' because, feeling an outcast socially and psychologically, uprooted from life in 'a more or less attenuated equivalent of death'.[18] But she goes on to point to the kind of hope that we have been discussing the hope that this misery may point to a presence beyond the perception of reason or common-sense, a meaning and a greater plenitude than the presence of all worldly entities, the 'things too wonderful for me, which I did not know'[19] which Job finally acknowledged and which justified his refusal to surrender his dignity. 'All the horrors produced

---

16. Weil, *Waiting For God*, 118–119
17. Kaufmann, 'In The Light Of "The light Of Transcendence"', 35.
18. *Job*, 42:3.
19. Weil, *Waiting For God*, 129.

in the world', Weil argues, 'are like the folds imposed on the waves by gravity'.[20] But beyond this physical necessity there is the necessity imposed by these 'things too wonderful' for us.

To many this may seem an unpalatable way of dealing with the problem of suffering. But it may be realistic. For Weil, just as 'one has to learn to read or to practice a trade, so one must learn to feel in all things . . . the obedience of the universe to God',[21] that is to some ultimate reality beyond our understanding. It seems to me that this is the insight offered by tragedy as well as by faith. To return to *If This Is A Man*, it is clear that Levi recovered hope when he caught a glimpse of this ultimately 'unreasonable reason' and that it was this which sustained and empowered him in his 'personal and secret battle against the camp and death', (p.143), enabling him to live, as Levinas puts it, with a 'full conscience [under an] empty sky'.[22]

---

20. Weil, *Waiting For God*, 131.
21. Weil, *Waiting For God*, 131.
22. Regina Schwartz, 'Revelation And Revolution', in *Cross Currents,* 56/3 (2006): 381–382

Death And Dying In Literature:
Human Dying In Literature:
Human Growth And Human Suffering

Let me begin with the proposition that it is not death but suffering which is the great problem. While it is true that death is all round us today, in the media it has become a kind of impersonal spectacle. In our personal lives, as one of the characters in Deborah Robinson's recent novel *Careless* says; "'Death has been torn from us . . . We are no longer able to look upon the dead in order to learn the lesson of our lives.'"[1] Contemplating the body of a young woman who has died from an overdose, he is 'suddenly struck by the mystery and melancholy of her face . . . Suddenly the beautiful girl she was became clear to me. All her torment had left her.' But there is also a sense of loss: "'I thought about how in other cultures people spent time with the dead, saying their goodbyes and helping them to cross over'".[2]

This may seem a disjointed opening to my reflections. So let me clarify the direction I want to take. Essentially I want to argue that our culture is unable to cope with the mystery of death. Emmanuel Levinas puts it this way: 'Modern man persists in his being as a sovereign who is concerned to maintain *the powers of his sovereignty* . . . Only by death is this sovereignty thwarted. The obstacle of death is insurmountable, inexorable and fundamentally incomprehensible.'[3] The novelist Patrick White puts it more spectacularly when his character Hurtle Duffield sees death as 'shapelessness'. A reality too big for us, like a 'kind of elephant.[4] Certainly it interrupts the stories we like to tell about ourselves and our place in the scheme of things and often seems to render them meaningless.

---

1. Deborah Robertson, *Careless* (Sydney: Picador, Pan Macmillan, 2006), 49.
2. Robertson, *Careless,* 53.
3. Sean Hand, *The Levinas Reader.* (Oxford: Wiley-Blackwell, 1993), 78.
4. Patrick White, *The Vivisector* (London: Cape, 1970), 40.

The fact is, however, that as another Australian writer Judith Wright wrote to a friend after the death of her life-long partner; 'Death's part of life, dammit'.[5] It is important therefore to discover stories which enable us better to come to terms with the realities of suffering and death and ways in which they may enable us to grow as human beings rather than destroy us. My central focus will be on Primo Levi's *If This Is A Man,* his account of his survival in a Nazi concentration camp.

If I am right in saying that it is not death but suffering which is the problem this book is important because it explores what may well be the ultimate kind of suffering, what Simone Weil calls 'affliction' which is not merely a matter of physical pain—though there is much of that in Levi's account, hunger, cold and exhaustion as well as brutal treatment by the guards—but something more profound, a sense of isolation, 'a more or less attenuated equivalent of death, irresistibly present to the *soul*', of being uprooted socially, psychologically and metaphysically from the human community, overwhelmed by forces beyond one's control and trapped in a world in which, as Levi put it, there seems to be 'no where or why'[6] beyond reason and without any hope of release. This may well be, as many of you will know, the way some people feel today facing death today.

But at this point let us leave Primo Levi for the moment to reflect on the way in which even in this situation it may be possible to preserve one's dignity. My evidence is the *Selected Poems* of Philip Hodgins, a young Australian who was in and out of hospital battling leukemia from 1983 when it was first diagnose until his death in 1995. His poems tell of the lonely journey he made to death, knowing that there was no cure and that, despite their love and care, friends and family

> in time will see me to the earth
> and stand around in groups and say
> expected things about this death.[7]

5.   Veronica Brady, *South of My Days: A Biography Of Judith Wright* (Sydney, Angus & Robertson, 1998), 215.

6.   Primo Levi, *Si C'est Un Homme* (Paris, Julliard, 1987), 34. A French translation of the Italian original *Se Questo E Un Uomo.* I am responsible for the translation from French into English

7.   Philip Hodgins, *Selected Poems* (Sydney, Angus & Robertson, 1997), 4.

and that

> there is no going back
> to the body's evanescent harmony (19)

but facing it steadily and without illusions, even without the defence of faith, writing, for instance, that

> as far as I can see, there is no God.(8)

Nor does he sentimentalise the care he is given: when the needle of the drip in his arm fell one night, the nurses who appeared, he felt, 'came to see / not me but it' (57). The impersonality of the care here contrasts with the sheer personal reality of his death.

In effect he plays his death as 'my most important piece' (4), playing the part given to him as best he can trying to 'be moderate for [his]friends' (46), for example, sometimes allowing self-pity but of an ironic kind—

> . . . I'm like the traveller
> on the kerb in a strange city, gaping—
> 'My dreams!
> I only put them down for a minute!' (20)—

but all the time carrying on a conversation with his antagonist death, 'summing each other up, trading ripostes and *bons mots*' (30) even as he faces his inevitable defeat, Happy, Sad. Sacred. Scared. Every day a different one as he lives 'out the whole thing in my mind', arriving at the conviction that it is not death which is

> . . . the overwhelming fact
> of our existence, but that moment when we find
> a link between our life and death, the final act (317).

It has always been the task literature to give death a certain kind of purity to render it personal and in that sense authentic and proper by rehearsing it, even as it accepts that our existence is finally beyond our control. As Herman Broch writes in *The Death Of Virgil:* 'Only he who accepted death was able to complete the circle of his mortality, only the eye of him who sought the eye of death would not fail when it gazed into nothingness',[8] the 'undiscover'd country from whose bourn/ No traveller returns', from which Hamlet shrank initially but which he finally entered so unflinchingly. Hodgins' poems also reveal a heroism which may well exceed the abilities of most of us. But his example and that of so many in literature who are able to 'gaze into nothingness' in this way is surely worth reflection.

But let us take a more comforting tack by returning to Primo Levi, to the moment to the moment which enabled him to endure and preserve his dignity the brutal world of the camp and find some meaning in the midst of its geometric madness'.[9] It happened in mid-winter and he and a fellow prisoner were carrying their daily food ration through the snow to the other prisoners in their hut when a passage from Dante's *Inferno* a turning point in his journey through hell which tells of the poet's meeting with Ulysses suddenly comes into his mind.

It is a poignant moment since Ulysses' description of the mountain he and his men saw on land as he and his men sailed through the Pillars of Hercules into the Atlantic reminds Levi of the mountain he used to see on his way home when he was a free man and the contrast between Ulysses' exhorting his men to follow him and not to deny the

> experience of that which lies beyond
> the sun, and of the world that is unpeopled (Canto XXVI,
> 116–117).

he is offering them as they break through into the ocean opening out before them increases Levi's anguish. Yet what happens next pulls him up short as Ulysses describes the way a sudden whirlwind strikes their ship tossing it around and finally sinking it. But what strikes Levi most is the conclusion of this description:

> so that our prow plunged deep, as pleased an Other (Canto
> XXVI, 141).

Linking it with Ulysses' words to his men as he urged them on that

> you were not meant to live your lives as brutes,
> but to be followers of worth and knowledge (Canto XXVI,
> 120-1).

---

8. Hermann Broch, *The Death Of Virgil,* translated by Jean Starr Untermeyer (New York: Random House Vintage International, 1995), 82.

9. Levi, *Si C'est Un Homme,* 64.

it seems to Levi that these words should speak to everyone who suffered but at this moment to him and his fellow prisoners in particular (149).

They also should concern us here, I suggest, especially if we recall what Simone Weil had to say about affliction, that essentially it involves a sense of uprootedness. Accepting Dante's implication that Ulysses is being punished for *hubris*, for defying the proper order of things, daring to go where no one else had been before, Levi glimpses an order beyond the 'geometric madness', (64) of the camp, an order whose ways might be beyond our comprehension in which suffering and death may no longer seem meaningless. Admitting that Dante's world view was very different from our and could easily be dismissed as merely 'medieval', he nevertheless senses its importance if they are not to 'live [their] lives as brutes' in the camp but continue to pursue 'worth and knowledge' and preserve their dignity even here.

It seems to me that this is the point made at the end of tragedies like *Hamlet* or of *Oedipus At Colonus* when after all his suffering Oedipus surrenders himself into the hands of the inscrutable gods. Similarly at the end of the *Book Of Job*, overwhelmed by the glimpse he has been given into the majestic power of creation Job bows down before 'things too wonderful for me, which I did not know' (*Job*, 42:3), accepts his limits even as he preserves his integrity. This is not to cancel out his suffering. But it is to confirm his conquest of affliction, the sense of meaninglessness which he has resisted throughout, and to look steadily at what Pascal calls the 'infinite immensity of spaces of which I am ignorant'.[10] This may seem bleak. But in the face of the inescapable realities of suffering and death, it may be that for most of us, as Theodor Adorno, who escaped from Hitler's Germany put it, hope lies in 'the concept of something that would differ from the unspeakable world that is'.[11]

Most cultures throughout human history have accepted this belief that, in the words Shakespeare's Prospero at the end of *The Tempest*; 'We are such stuff as dreams are made, on and our little lives/ Are rounded with a sleep' and that we need some kind of belief in this order if we are to avoid despair. Our present Western culture seems to

10. Blaise Pascal, *Pensees,* in Mack, Maynard *et al*, editors, *World Masterpieces* (New York: Norton, 1965), 32.

11. Wayne Cristaudo, Wayne and Wendy Baker, editors, *Messianism Apocalypse & Redemption In 20ᵗʰ Century Thought* (Adelaide: ATF Press, 2006), 41.

be the exception with many people unable to accept the existence of any realities beyond our understanding or beyond the possibilities of our control. This is not the place for theological argument, especially as my time is running out. So let me suggest briefly what this kind of belief may have to contribute to our considerations.

To see death as the interface between this world and another which is beyond our comprehension is to give death a meaning, even perhaps a purpose—at least to the person dying. One Jewish thinker Nachman of Breslov put it this way:

> The entire world is a very narrow bridge
> The most important thing is not to be afraid.[12]

and literature is full of examples of those who made their way across this bridge with courage and dignity people in whose lives, to quote Shakespeare once more, nothing became them as much as their leaving of it. What of those who care for them, however? Obviously we cannot go with them. But here Deborah Robertson's *Careless* has important things to say as it deals the ways in which, like one of her characters, we react to death, telling herself that the 'wager with is own mortality' in which the man she loves is 'something private' which 'she did not wish to see'.[13](Robertson 2006: 100) and turning away from it to protect herself. Another character, a young and ambitious artist tries to build his reputation by trying to anaesthetise death, arguing that 'once you had beauty, you had redemption'.[14] Yet the novel makes clear that this is to fail what may be the crucial test of our humanity, that as Martin Heidegger (argued,[15] to fail to understand and accept our mortality, the 'unconcealedness' of the realities of pain, death and love is a sign of human destitution. And that may be the deepest suffering that afflicts a culture which shrinks from death.

---

12. Fran Gale, Natalie Bolzan and Dorothy McRae-McMahon editors, *Spirited Practices: Spirituality and The Helping Professions* (Sydney: Allen & Unwin, 2007), 51.

13. Deborah Robertson, *Careless* (Sydney: Picador, Pan Macmillan, 2006), 100

14. Robertson, *Careless*, 123.

15. Matin Heidegger, *Poetry, Language, Thought* (New York: Harper Colophon Books, 1975), 95–96.

All That is Solid Melts Into the Air: Australia's Future?

My title, of course, comes from Karl Marx's discussion of the effects of the Industrial Revolution. But it is not a far-fetched reference, I believe, when applied to a settler society like Australia, 'last sea thing dredged by Sailor Time for Space'[1] as far as its effects are concerned, since our arrival has had similar effects, damaging if not dissolving relationships built up over thousands of years between the land and its Aboriginal inhabitants and imposing on it a model developed elsewhere—in my view with disastrous consequences for both.

Mircea Eliade argues that settlement in a hitherto unknown land involves more than material and economic development and that the consequences are also imaginative since the 'transformation of chaos into cosmos' needs to be given a form which makes it become real'.[2] In traditional societies this transformation has, by and large, been largely positive. But from the beginnings faced with a strange and difficult environment, we have tended to suspect what is unseen and indefinable. In 1904, for example, AG Stevens noted that 'there is in the developing Australian character a sceptical and utilitarian spirit that values the present hour and refuses to sacrifice for the present for any visionary future lacking a rational guarantee'. Attempting to mould an untouched and often intransigent environment to their will, the settlers 'had little time or energy to spare for metaphysical speculation, feeling what they achieved, they owed to themselves, and

---

1. Bernard O'Dowd, 'Australia', in HP Heseltine, editor, *The Penguin Book of Australian Verse* (Ringwood, Vic: Penguin Press, 1979), 95.
2. Mircea Eliade, *The Myth of the Eternal Return or, Cosmos and History* (Princeton: Princeton University Press, 1974), 113.

found little for which to thank their fathers heaven',[3] and is much the same today, I believe.

By and large our energies are still devoted to material and economic development and in many respects we remain, as AD Hope put it, 'second hand Europeans' who 'populate timidly on the edge of alien shores'.[4] Yet the task of imagining ourselves into existence in this strange new land—two hundred years is a very short time in world history—is both challenging and necessary. In this paper, therefore, I would like to explore two attempts, two attempts to imagine ourselves into existence. One is Joseph Furphy's, *Such is Life*,[5] published in 1903, and the other David Malouf's more recent *An Imaginary Life*, which was published in 1978.

Such is Life, is the more explicit in its attempt to discover our place in the larger scheme of things, to develop some kind of cosmic understanding to enable us resist the pressures of this new place. Its opening scene has a cosmic setting which conveys a sense of our human vulnerability with the narrator and central character, Tom Collins, finding himself unemployed, speculating that this may have been predestined 'ever since a scrap of fire-mist flew from the solar centre from our planet' (1) decided to fill in his time by setting down the events of a week in his life as a government official in the outback before the coming of the railway when goods and supplies had been transported by teams of bullocks.

Most novelists set their characters in a social context. But here society seems to have dissolved, leaving the individual solitary and exposed to the powers of nature. The novel's opening scene describes a solitary horseman riding across the Riverina plains 'between earth and sky' and the 'geodesic dome' of the firmament with the sun blazing 'wastefully and thanklessly down' (2) and concludes on a similar cosmic note with a parody of Macbeth's despairing 'tomorrow and tomorrow and tomorrow' speech: such is life my fellow mummers— just like a poor player, that bluffs and feints his hour upon the stage, and than cheapens down to mere nonentity' (297).

---

3. Ian Turner (editor), The Australian Dream (Melbourne: Sun Books, 1968), x–xi

4. AD Hope, 'Australia', in HP Heseltine, *The Penguin Book*, 190.

5. John Barnes, editor, *Portable Australian Authors: Joseph Furphy* (St Lucia QLD: University of Queensland Press), 19. Hereafter all page references will be given in the text.

In this pioneering world the public realm and the 'power of illumination' it usually offers[6] no longer seem to exist. The self is alone in an indifferent and often hostile world. As Tom puts it later: 'We are all walking along the shelving edge of a precipice and any one of us may go at any time or be dragged down by another' (94). Furphy's characters, mostly bullock drivers, live and work on the fringes of society, carrying supplies and produce to and from remote stations, must rely on their wits to survive, often at odds with the squatters they serve since their bullocks need grass and most squatters will not let them graze on their properties so that the drivers have to break into the squatters' land to let their bullocks feed there.

So the drivers' lives tend to involve a series of 'dirty transactions'. As one of them says wearily to Tom:

> The world's full of dirty transactions and it's a dirty transaction to round up a man's team in a ten-mile paddock, and stick a bob a head on them, but that's a thing that I'm very familiar with; it's a dirty transaction to refuse water to perishing beasts, but I've been refused times out of number and will be to the end of the chapter, it's a dirty transaction to persecute men for having no occupation but carting, yet that's what one-tenths of the squatter's do (13).

Working and living as they do more or less as outlaws, they find brief moments of community in the evening in chance encounters with other travellers around the camp fire sharing stories, mostly about survival in a harsh and indifferent land which has little or no sympathy for or with human beings or indeed, their animals. As a result they must accommodate themselves to the land as best they can by transforming the chaos' facing them into 'cosmos' by finding some 'latent meaning' in it, 'so grave, subdued, self-centred; so alien to the genial appeal of more winsome landscape' and interrupting it 'faithfully ad lovingly' (65). But this meaning lies beyond common-sense, pointing to the larger, more mysterious, reality hinted at in the descriptions in the early scene of a group around a campfire at night:

---

6. Rene Pascal, 'Pensées' in Maynard Mack *et al* (editors), World Masterpieces II (New York: WW Norton & Company, 1965), 32.

> It was a clear but moonless night; the dark blue canopy spangled with myriad stars—grandeur, peace and purity above; squalor, worry, and profanity below. Fit basis for many a system of theology—unscientific, if you will, but by no means contemptible (13)

One is reminded here of Prospero's vision in *The Tempest*:

> ... We are such stuff
> As dreams are made on and our little lives
> Are rounded with a sleep

And also of Paschal's *Pensées 265:*

> When I consider the short duration of my life, swallowed up in the eternity before and after, the little space which I fill, and even can see, engulfed in the infinite immensity of spaces of which I am ignorant, and which know me not, I am frightened and astonished at being here rather than there, for there is no reason why here rather than there.[7]

For them, therefore, identity become and anxious matter. As Luis Carlos points out traditional societies identify is a 'closed circle around sameness'.[8] This closed circle in which the self 'triumphs above all as critical understanding, distinguishing and identifying good and evil in a very particular way, based on itself, on its glorious position as basis and referent of the whole of reality spread outs its feet' (80). Whereas, in contrast, in settler societies, initially at least, the self is a pilgrim to some elsewhere beyond the horizon rather than a figure like Ulysses who is trying to find his way home or to re-establish it there, as many more privileged settlers in this country tried, to 'build a New Britannia in another world', as WC Wentworth put it in the early days in New South Wales.

Such is Life, is, I suggest, a 'pilgrim text' of this kind since in it Furphy explores the possibility of better kind of society than the one we have at present, one which provides a 'fair go' for all. So, as he says, it is a novel whose 'temper' was 'democratic and its "bias" offensively Australian', attempting to dissolve established forms and practices.

---

7. Luiz Carlos Susin 'A Critique of the Identity Paradigm', *Concilium* (2002/2): 87
8. Ian Turner, *The Australian Dream*, 12.

There is not the space to explore any further what he has to say on this score, though it is worth pointing out that, as we have already noted, he anticipates some of the metaphysical concerns evident in the works of later writers like Patrick White and Randolph Stow. Instead let us turn to David Malouf's work, *An Imaginary Life*, which was published in 1978.[9]

As the contrast between the two titles implies, stylistically it is very different from *Such is Life*, much shorter, less argumentative and more of an idyll, what Bakhtin called a 'chronotype of threshold' since it combines the motif of encounter with a crisis or break in life which expands the reader's sense of reality. It is about a 'wild child' brought up by animals in the wilderness. But its protagonist, is sophisticate, Ovid, the Roman poet who has been banished by the Emperor to the fringes of the civilised world to live among the tribal people there who becomes aware of a 'latent meaning' to be found here.

But for Malouf, this meaning is metaphysical rather than political or social, as it was for Furphy and comes from beyond the self, 'the unknown' into which the 'Wild Child' he encounters there finally leads him to follow 'the clear path if [his] fate', to push out beyond the merely human, 'beyond what know cannot by my limits' (135). In that sense he can be seen as a Promethean figure. Nevertheless the tone is 'feminine', receptive rather than 'masculine' and aggressive— as it is in *Such is Life*—since he is responding to a call from beyond the self which is to transform it.

Significantly the real life Ovid shared this preoccupation in Ovid, in his major work, the *Metamorphoses*. As *An Imaginary Life* concludes Ovid is following the Wild Child, identifying with him with the 'immensity of the landscape' and caught up in a life beyond history and 'beyond the limits of measurable time' (144). If we turn to the question facing a settler society like ours, it could then be said that, properly seen, colonial identity ought not to be a 'closed circle around sameness',[10] a replication of the work from which we have come. But, Malouf suggests, a continual series of beginnings, painful settings out into the unknown, 'pushing off from the edges of consciousness into the mystery of what we have not yet except in

9.   David Malouf, *An Imaginary Life* (London: Chatto & Windus, 1978). Hereafter all references will be given in the text.
10. Susin, 'A Critique', 88.

in dreams' (135), dreams which will enable us to live in tune with the universe—in contrast with *Such is Life* in which, as we have seen, a tension exists between the self and nature.

In this way, I suggest, An Imaginary life, may have something significant to say to us as Australians about the task of settlement which is still to be achieved, which is to move beyond the limits of the imperial imagination and, to draw on the distinction made by Heidegger, learn from its 'First Peoples' who have lived in and with this land so long, intimately and respectfully, learn how to 'dwell' in it rather than merely to 'build' on it, exploiting it for our own purposes.

History, Eternity And Identity.
Paul Cox's *Man Of Flowers*

Any work of art, or indeed of imagination, has a two-fold character: it is at one and the same time autonomous and social fact in its creation but also in its reception. Paul Cox was well aware of this, remarking in an interview that a film is a political act as well. But for a film maker of his remarkable independence and integrity his films are also profoundly personal: politics has to do with human aspirations and relationships. So I want to discuss his early masterpiece *Man Of Flowers* as an example of this interplay between the personal and the political, time and the timeless, using the film, to keep this focus steady.

Its opening moments are crucial: a dark forest momentarily lit by rays of light. One may be reminded here perhaps of the dark wood in which Dante began his journey through the *Inferno* and *Purgatorio* to *Paradiso* but also of Cox's own childhood memory of walking with his father into a dark wood which was suddenly illuminated by a shaft of light. The sound-track here (which runs right through the action) is in tune with this journey since it is from *Lucia di Lammermoor,* an opera about love struggling to survive in dark times—as Cox was also, born in 1942 in Holland, then under occupation by Nazi Germany. In the foreground of this opening scene, however, there is a solitary figure, a man clothed in black wearing a ruff reminiscent of Picasso's drawing of Don Quixote, the hero who to the end of his life continued to 'dream the impossible dream' of a world in which a village prostitute appeared as a princess and windmills as giants, the kind of world described in two of the epigraphs to Patrick White's novel *The Solid Mandala* (whose main protagonist, Arthur Brown, was engaged in a similar quest) Paul Eluard's 'There is another world, but it is in this one' and Meister Eckhart's 'It is not outside but inside: wholly within'.

The next frame, however, returns us to the maelstrom of history. It is a shot of the grey waves of the sea—a *leit motif* which runs through Cox's work as an image of transition and often also of estrangement—as it is here, visually echoing the loneliness of Matthew Arnold's poem, 'Dover Beach', set on the shore of the English Channel which separates the solitary figure standing there from the French woman he loves listening to

> Its melancholy, long, withdrawing roar,
> Retreating, to the breath
> Of the night wind, down the vast edges drear
> And naked shingles of the world.

But in the film this sea imagery, I suspect, also leads us to WB Yeats' 'Sailing To Byzantium', a poem about the journey he must take across the seas from a world in which the 'aged man' he is becoming

> . . . is but a paltry thing,
> A tattered cloak upon a stick, unless
> Soul clap its hands and sing, and louder sing
> For every tatter in its mortal dress,

to 'the holy city of Byzantium', the city of art, to stand in the great cathedral of Sancta Sophia, (Sacred Wisdom) and stand before the mosaics of 'the sages standing in God's holy fire', beseeching them to 'be the singing masters of my soul'.[1]

This, I suggest, is the world and the journey with which Cox's films are concerned, and especially so in *Man of Flowers*. This is not surprising, however, if we reflect on the world into which Cox was born, the Europe described by Heinrich Blucher, Hannah Arendt's partner (who had managed to escape with her from that world to the safety of New York) as 'a social maelstrom, driven by interests . . . [sucking] us down into the depths' which had smashed into Europe, creating a 'boiling mass a society of ghostlike, isolated individuals [afflicted by the deluded belief] that history is being made directly here' and intent on moving 'directly from the past to the future by leaping over the present, as if [Blucher observes] a future could ever open up for human beings who have lost sight of eternity.[2]

---

1. WB Yeats, *Collected Poems* (London: Macmillan, 1971), 217.
2. *Correspondence Hannah Arendt Karl Jaspers 1926–1969,* edited by Lotte Kohler and Hans Saner (New York: Harcourt Brace Harvest Book, 1992), 278.

Such 'ghostlike isolated individuals' abound in Cox's films and in *Man Of Flowers* also. Chief of them in this film is the angry ghost of the boy friend of Charles Bremer's 'little flower', a second-rate artist with little sense of anything apart from his own imagined genius, drugs, sex and money. We are also introduced to a melancholy psychiatrist overwhelmed by the sadness of things and, more positively, the postman who figures as a kind Greek chorus, arriving every morning to announce that 'the world is fucked', but manages, however, to take up arms against this sea of troubles with his cheerful sociability.

But it is the search for eternity, for what TS Eliot in *Four Quartets* calls 'the still point of the turning world' which is 'both a new world and the old made explicit'[3] which is central. In *Man Of Flowers*, though at first he may seem one of these 'ghostlike isolated individuals', Charles Bremer, the film's central character, a solitary figure dressed in black living alone in a large house is in fact not one of them since he has not lost sight of eternity and is in many respects a kind of Don Quixote, insisting on the glimpse he caught as a child in the beauty of his mother's body, and writing to her every day and refusing to accept that she is dead. To keep the dream alive he contrives a vision of this paradise once a week in a room filled with flowers in his home as a young woman, his 'little flower', ceremonially disrobes before him to display the splendour of her body.

The iconography here, the flowers and the mandala shape on the wall behind her—which could be seen as the monstrance in which the consecrated host is displayed in the traditional Roman Catholic ceremony of Benediction—makes this is a sacred moment like the vision of 'the Love that moves the sun and the other stars' which concludes Dante's *Paradiso*. Like Dante's it is a vision of innocence, of paradise regained in a 'world within this world, but that which is not world'—to quote Eliot once more—a moment of liberation which consists

> . . . not in movement
> But abstention from movement; while the world moves
> In appetency, on its metalled ways
> Of time past and future.[4]

---

3. TS Eliot, *Four Quartets* (London: Faber & Faber, 1954), 9.
4. Eliot, *Four Quartets*, 11.

Which released him from the violence of history into 'real time'. In an attempt to prolong the moment therefore, as his 'little flower' dresses again to return to the everyday world, he hurries from his house to the church opposite to sit down at the organ and play out his joy on the organ so loudly and with such passion that the vicar, coming in at that moment, remarks that 'the whole church is quivering, to which Bremer replies; 'Yes, I know'.

We are getting ahead of ourselves, however. Before we explore these implications any further we should return to the dark forest of the opening scene and to the frame which follows it, the glimpse of the grey waves of the ocean which, we have already suggested, sounds a further note of estrangement. But the fact that sea imagery of this kind occurs frequently in Cox's work suggests another personal reference, that this image may express the sadness of leaving home, as Cox and so many of his of his generation felt obliged to do in order to escape from what Patrick White (who was at much the same time leaving London to return to Australia) described as 'the Gothic shell of Europe . . . in which the ghosts of Homer and St Paul and Tolstoy sat waiting for the crash'[5] in search of 'the state of silence, simplicity and humility' he had known there from time to time as a child growing up on the land.[6]

Both artists, it seems, were driven by a tension they felt between the world in which they found themselves, the 'Old World' and a new one which, in the words of Theodor Adorno, would be 'different from the unspeakable world that is,[7] the physical and spiritual desolation which is the legacy of war. Whether or not in real life Cox could have articulated it in these terms is beside the point I am trying to make here, which is to suggest that a similar quest for innocence, for a 'world wholly within' and therefore invulnerable is the refuge, is Charles Bremer's goal in *Man Of Flowers* since it offers an alternative to the world in which we live, the world of 'appetency' as it moves 'on its metalled ways' in which we live.

There is nothing sentimental, I would argue, about the way in which the film presents this search since it is for a wholeness which is also a kind of holiness, a state which is hard-earned and can damage

---

5. Patrick White, *The Aunt's Story* (London: Eyre & Spottiswoode, 1969), 146.

6. Patrick White, 'The Prodigal Son', *Australian Letters*, I, (1958): 37.

7. David Kaufman, 'In Light Of "The Light Of Transcendence": Redemption In *Adorno*', in Wayne Cristaudo and Wendy Baker, editors, *Messianism Apocalypse & Redemption in 20th Century Thought* (Adelaide: ATF Press, 2006), 41.

those who pursue it. Bremer is an incomplete and isolated human being and his relationship with his 'little flower', a purely imaginary one, alienates him still further from human community and finally drives him to murder her boy-friend, though with characteristic eccentricity since he kills his victim with poisoned darts which he notices in the antique shop he frequents and disposes of the body by encasing it in metal and turning it into a statue in his garden.

Bremer's relationship with his 'little flower' is also regarded ironically. For him she is a figure of vulnerable innocence, as Beauty exploited by the Beast, her boy-friend. But it is clear that in their quarrels she able to give as good as she gets and finally declares her independence from him to set up a lesbian relationship with one of her women friends. In effect for all its aesthetic beauty, the film implies that utopia does not exist and we must do the best with what we have.

At the same time the dream of a different kind of world remains here as in Cox's films which can be seen as an attempt to keep the dream alive. Innocence also seems a way of doing so, and I am reminded here of Adorno's comparison of this quest to 'a child at the piano searching for a chord never previously heard', knowing intuitively, however, that this chord must exist 'since the possible combinations are limited and actually everything that can be played on it is implicitly given in the keyboard'. This is a Romantic position, of course. Not yet part of our culture of suspicion, the child still has 'intimations of immortality', still catches glimpses of glory—as Cox's films do.

But that, I believe, does not make them escapist or irrelevant, at least if we take the point Adorno goes on to make, that the kind of utopia we are discussing may involve 'the negation of what exists' but it is nevertheless by definition 'obedient to it'[8] since it is what it has to work with. For that reason, as he argues, in the final paragraph of his *Minima Moralia,* a series of reflections written during World War II and in its immediate aftermath that 'the only philosophy that can be responsibly practised in the face of despair is the attempt to contemplate all things as they would present themselves from the standpoint of redemption'. In comparison with the hope which this attempt generates, 'the reality or unreality of redemption itself hardly matters.'[9]

---

8. John Hughes, 'Unspeakable Utopia: Art And The Return To Theological In Adorno And Horkheimer', in *Cross Currents* 53/4 (Winter, 2004), 478.

9. Theodor Adorno, *Minima Moralia* (London: Verso, 1994), 247.

Seen in this light it seems to me that *Man Of Flowers* and indeed Cox's work as a whole has important things to say about the possibilities that a new country like Australia might have had to offer to him and others like him as they turned their backs on an old world in ruins. For him it seems to have been what we may call a sacramental sense of reality which enabled him to trust rather than distrust the appearances and from time to time find the ideal becoming real in them and vice versa—a radical and transformative possibility in a world which increasingly tends as Jean Baudrillard puts it, to rest on 'the exaltation of signs based on the denial of the reality of things'.[10]

But this insight also makes him important as a film-maker since this tension between signs and the reality of things has always weighed heavily on artists in the field, especially, I suppose, on someone as preoccupied with the possibility of redemption from the merely natural realm of necessity and law as Cox has been. That is why *Man Of Flowers* seems to me such an achievement in the way in which he has managed to preserve the autonomy and visionary quality of his art and at the same time to pay his dues to social and historical fact. Suburban Melbourne has seldom seemed more significant and fascinating than it does here but also more recognisable.

This is clear, for example, in the lead in to the ecstatic disrobing scene which in which Bremer's 'little flower' emerges from her boy friend's squalid studio to walk down a slum lane on her way to her appointment with him. Acknowledging the tension between the two worlds in this way, however, serves to intensify the scene's dramatic force and gives it credibility. Cox is also careful, as we have seen, not to sentimentalise his characters and the situations in which they find themselves, ironically undercutting the figure of Bremer, for instance, even as he builds towards the tragi-comic pathos of history's conclusion. Where he might have been merely a pathetic figure of an unhappy child who becomes a lonely man, wealthy and privileged but friendless or a moralistic counterpoint to the preoccupation with what DH Lawrence described as 'the business of money-making, money-having and money-spending' so much admired in our culture, at the end the comically impossible nature of his revenge on his beloved's boy-friend undercuts the pathos of his existence, reminding us that in the long run wealth and privilege, like art, cannot substitute for the

---

10. Jean Baudrillard, *Revenge Of The Crystal: Selected Essays On The Modern Object And Its Destiny, 1968–1983* (Sydney: Pluto Press, 1990), 63.

complex pains and pleasures of everyday life. Bremer remains, like Don Quixote, a hero only in his dreams.

So it is clear, that no matter how many letters he writes to her, the fact is that Bremer's adored mother is dead. Similarly, although as a child he rages against his father and aims shanghai at him, his paternal power cannot be destroyed and his mother ultimately belongs to him. His hold on his 'little flower' is even more fragile, a mere one-sided fantasy. To begin with, as far as she is concerned the relationship is only a way of earning money to support her boy friend's need for drugs. But as time goes by, she finds the situation increasingly puzzling, coming to realise that, despite the appearances, he has no intention of seducing her but is 'a good man'. But this only leads her to pity him for his loneliness and isolation, so that in the long run there is no mutual understanding or real interaction between them. Instead she leaves him behind in her new relationship with the woman with whom she shares understanding as well as love.

To conclude, then, *Man Of Flowers* offers us an ironic vision of the human condition which is nevertheless a deeply sympathetic one, not unlike the classic vision Alexander Pope proposes in his 'Essay On Man' of a creature

> Placed on this isthmus of a middle state,
> A being darkly wise, and rudely great . . .
> . . . The glory, jest, and riddle of the world!

Yet at the same time it honours the world of Don Quixote, the world also of Shakespeare's Prospero in *The Tempest* for whom

> . . . We are such stuff
> As dreams are made on, and our little lives
> Are rounded with a sleep.

We remain in the dark forest of existence in which the film began. But Don Quixote is still there, dreaming still that, as Adorno suggests also, what we call 'reality' is not yet 'real' that the rifts and cracks within the world of appearances are able, however briefly, and the shafts of light that occasionally strike through them enable us from time to time to 'rehearse the right life'[11] and keep alive the hope of some final redemption from the maelstrom of history.

---

11. Theodor Adorno, *Minima Moralia,* 228

The Dragon Slayer:
Patrick White And The Contestation of History

Let me use two quotations to frame my argument. The first is from Nietzsche's *Twilight Of The Idols*, an attack on commonsense, what is generally seen as 'the 'true world' which he dismissed as an 'idea which is no longer good for anything, not even obligating—an idea which has become useless and superfluous—*consequently*, a refuted idea: let us abolish it!'[1] The second is Adorno's claim that transcendence, properly understood and pursued, enables thought to 'converge upon something that would differ from the unspeakable world that is'.[2] A strain that is at once utopian and dystopian runs through Australian culture, as it does through most colonial cultures and these two quotations speak to the tension between the two apparent in the work of Patrick White and also to the way he negotiates it.

In his case it was intensified his personal circumstances. Born in London in 1912 to a Privileged Australian pastoral family who regarded England as 'home', he spent the first part of his life oscillating between the two sides of the world, suspended between belonging and alienation, beginning his education in Australia, for instance, but completing at an English Public School and later at Cambridge. Having spent his vacations in Germany in the years immediately before World War II he seems to have shared WH Auden's sense of living in 'low, sick, dishonest decade', the decade of the Great Depression, the rise of Fascism and Nazism, Stalin's Show Trials, the Spanish Civil

---

1. Frederick Nietzsche, 'The Twilight Of The Idols', in *The Portable Nietzsche,* edited by Walter Kaufmann (Ringwood Vic: Penguin Books, 1981), 485.
2. David Kaufmann, 'In The Light Of Transcendence: Redemption In Adorno', in *Messianism Apocalypse & Redemption In 20ᵗʰ Century German Thought,* edited by Wayne Cristaudo and Wendy Baker (Adelaide, ATF Press, 2006), 41.

War and the bombing of Guernica and a general feeling that, as EM Forster wrote, some incalculable malevolence seemed to be assailing the human mind, 'the prelude to an incalculable catastrophe in the whole of Western civilisation'.[3]

White's first publication, *The Ploughman And Other Poems*, echoes these Apocalyptic feelings. One poem, for instance, describes 'the moon's silver-papered kite' falling 'in tatter on a cloud.[4] Later when war came his service as an intelligence officer in the Royal Air Force in the Western desert gave him fresh images of disaster and returning on leave to London during the Blitz did little to relieve them. It seems important therefore to situate his subsequent work in this context, not only for the light it throws on his artistic project as a whole but also for the reasons for his return to Australia and then on the problematic reception of his work, especially in the early years after his return. His aesthetic concerns were at odds with what he attacked as the 'dun coloured realism'[5] of Australian writing of the time. They were preoccupied with the 'true world' which Nietzsche and those influenced by him rejected, where *The Living And The Dead* suggests that he was searching for the reality Nietzsche saw as 'unattainable for now, but promised for the sage, the pious, the virtuous man, ("for the sinner who repents").'[6]

The mutual misunderstanding involved is apparent, for example, in Kylie Tennant's review of *Voss*: 'When the book strikes off into the deserts of mysticism [she wrote], I am one of those people who would sooner slink off home.'[7] But she was not alone. Other critics were obviously uneasy with White's metaphysical concerns. Peter Woods was typical when he complained of an absence in White's novels of 'issues we can take seriously at an adult level'[8]—metaphysics apparently being something adults outgrow. Many, if not most critics were also uneasy with White's prose style which also worked to

3. EM Forster, 'After Munich', in *Two Cheers For Democracy* (London: Hogarth Press, 1951), 23.
4. Patrick White, *The Ploughman And Other Poems* (Sydney: Beacon Press, 1935), 11.
5. 'The Prodigal Son', *Australian Letters*. I, 3 (Sydney 1958), 37.
6. Walter Kaufmann, *The Portable Nietzsche*, 485.
7. Kylie Tennant, "Poetic Symbolism In Novel By Patrick White." *Sydney Morning Herald*, 8th February, 1958: 12
8. Peter Wood, 'Moral Complexity In Patrick White's Novels', in *Meanjin*, XXI (1962): 22.

interrogate commonsense by its attempt to fuse outer perception with inner feeling: AD Hope famously characterised it as 'pretentious and illiterate verbal sludge'.[9] In return White was to pillory such people, and *Voss*, written some time after his return, rests on the distinction it draws between Mr Bonner and his friends who believe only in what they can see, touch and calculate and cling to the fringes of the self as they cling to the fringes of the continent, wanting only to be 'safe in life, safe in death'[10] and those prepared to make the journey into the interior with the explorer Voss, into the deserts of the real. Why, then, did he decide to return?

The Aunt's Story, written on his way home and published in London in 1948, the year of White's return, described Europe as 'gothic shell . . . the aching wilderness in which the ghosts of Homer, St Paul and Tolstoy waited for the crash'.[11] The austerity of the landscape of Greece where he spent time immediately after the war and its austerity had reminded him of the Australian landscape he had known as a child which seemed to promise the "state of silence, simplicity and humility" which he now regarded as the only proper state for the artist but also for any human being.[12] The Europe from which he wanted to escape was the product of the culture which, Karl Jaspers was arguing at this time, had endowed history with a 'false grandeur . . . stolen from God'.[13] But this grandeur had lead to the 'aching wilderness' White sensed around him, leading him, as Adorno put it, to look to create 'something that would differ from the unspeakable world that is',[14] a new sense of self and of reality which would contest 'the triumph of radical evil'.[15] For White Australia which he imagined as somehow beyond history might be the place to make this attempt.

His attempt to realise this hope has been extensively explored. But so far there has been little discussion of the pressures which brought it about, their influence on his subsequent career and the challenge they implied to the culture to which he returned which was essentially

---

9. AD Hope.
10. Patrick White, *Voss* (Ringwood, Vic: Penguin, 1971), 349.
11. Patrick White, *The Aunt's Story* (London, Eyre & Spottiswoode, 1969), 146.
12. White, "The Prodigal Son", 35.
13. Lotte Kohler and Hans Saner, editors, *Correspondence Hannah Arendt Karl Jaspers 1926-1969.* (New York: Harcourt Brace Harvester Book, 1993), 149.
14. Kaufmann, *The Portable Nietzsche,* 41
15. Kaufmann, *The Portable Nietzsche,* 47.

pragmatic and materialist and addicted to the imperial history which had created it. But, consciously or unconsciously, White brought with him the desire to rescue the power of what Adorno called 'semblance' on which thinkers many European thinkers of the time were appealing in an attempt to negate current commonsense.[16] White's second novel *The Living And The Dead,* published in 1941, centres on this kind of response to the 'maelstrom' of history which Heinrich Blucher described seemed smashing into the world, creating 'a boiling mass society of ghostlike, isolated individuals',[17] a world 'under the spell of death and terror' in which understanding was 'frozen and naturalised . . . in a *still life* or landscape'.[18]

That is the landscape White's novel describes also, opening on a note of alienation and loss with Elyot Standish saying goodbye to his sister—significantly named Eden--who is leaving England to fight to take part in the war in Spain {in which her lover has been killed) and, noticing nearby a young Jewish woman whose husband is returning to Europe, is drawn 'into a region where the present dissolved its forms and purposes became a shapeless, directionless well of fear'. Soon afterwards on his way home he watches 'anchored where he stood . . . the audience to a piece of distant pantomime', as a drunk, as if 'walking with his eyes shut'[19] lurches under a bus. We are situated in a place which is no-place--if we accept the definition of 'place' as "space imbued with meaning'[20]—the equivalent of Sartre's *huis clos,* a dead end in which Elyot feels he has no 'power to restore a pretence of life' (8).

This sense of fatedness, waste and disgust, pervades the novel. True, Eden rebels against it and in this sense foreshadows the direction White's work and perhaps also the direction his life was to take later. Where Elyot remains a helpless spectator, she is prepared to take a stand and contest the situation, breaking out of her middle-

---

16. Kaufmann, *The Portable Nietzsche,* 42.

17. Kohler and Saner, 278.

18. Michael Taussig, *Walter Benjamin's Grave:*(London: University of Chicago Press, 2006), 27

19. Patrick White, *The Living And The Dead* (Ringwood, Vic: Penguin, 1967), 10. References hereafter will be given in the text of the essay

20. Frank Vanclay, "Place Matters", in Frank Vanclay, Matthew Higgins and Adam Blackshaw, editors, *Making Sense Of Place* (Canberra, National Museum of Australia, 2008), 3.

class enclosure with her working class love Joe Barnett for whom the sufferings of the Spanish people 'got to being part of [himself]' (307) so that he decided to fight with them in Spain. But he is killed there and even though she then decides to go herself to Spain her earlier confession to Joe implies that this is a futile gesture. She is 'sick of politics, the political lie' and no longer believes 'in the parties of politics', she tells him. What she wants is 'a change from wrong to right, which has nothing to do with category . . . I want to unite those who have the capacity for living, in any circumstance, and make it the one circumstance . . . [and to]oppose them to the dealers in words, to the diseased, to the most fatally diseased—the indifferent. That can be the only order . . . [since it is] without ideological limits. Labels set a limit at once. And there is no limit to man (253–254).

In the context of the novel these are mere words which have no effect. The novel belongs to Elyot and his story ends where it began, trapped in a circle of futility, as just returned from the station, he leaves home again to take a bus 'bound for nowhere in particular' (358). White was later embarrassed by this novel and not surprisingly little attention has been paid to it. Yet on the one hand the profound disgust with the direction history was taking evident in it illuminates his decision to return to Australia and on the other, overblown as it is, Eden's declaration points in the direction he was to take, his desire to transcend history and the hope which inspired it, the belief Hannah Arendt expressed that 'the one great opportunity' to change its disastrous course lay in an appeal to 'human existence itself, remaining loyal to reality though good and ill'.[21]

What 'reality', means, of course, then becomes the crucial question. Certainly, the world *The Living And The Dead* describes is not real, and not worthy of this reality. It is a mere world of appearances in which the self is inauthentic and emotionally frozen. Even as a child, for example, when Elyot is told of his father's death in World War he stands looking out into the garden, seeing every object clearly but feeling, only that 'he had no part in anything' (110). As White remarked in his autobiographical essay, 'The Prodigal Son', however, 'there is nothing like a rain of bombs to set one thinking'[22] and also, it seems, feeling. His war experience brought him face to face with

---

21. Kohler and Saner, 283.
22. White, "The Prodigal Son", 35

death: as an Intelligence Officer in the Western Desert, for example, he was required to search the enemy dead for possible strategic information and the London Blitz to which he returned on leave confronted him with the destruction of a city. In contrast, as we have seen, his memories of the Australian landscape seemed to promise a new beginning.

Ironically, in first novel *Happy Valley,* published in 1939, it had appeared as 'the land of plagues . . . only not so full of allegory',[23] a place whose inhabitants had most frighteningly failed to take hold of life, a failed utopia of a sick civilisation. But the aesthetic concerns which emerge in *The* Living *And The Dead* offered a glimpse of an alternative to the miserable world it described and thus paved the way for his return to Australia. So it may be worth reflecting on them here. I suspect they had something to do with his time at Cambridge since he was a member of King's College where the novelist EM Forster was a Fellow during White's time there and the influence of GE Moore's philosophy on which Forster's aesthetic rested was strong.

For Moore the good is indefinable, a matter of intuitive experience, to be perceived in personal relationships or in response to beautiful objects. Consequently the most desirable states are of a semi-mystical nature, moments of deep self-consciousness to which social organisation is at best irrelevant and at worst inimical. These ideas were central to the Bloomsbury Group which included writers like Virginia and Leonard Woolf, artists like Clive Bell and public figures like Maynard Keynes. As a young 'colonial' White would not have had anything to do with them. But his friendship with the painter Roy le Maistre after he came down from Cambridge would probably have made him made aware of these ideas, however little the interest he had or claimed to have in philosophy. The belief that, as Forster put it, art is 'the one orderly product which our muddling race has produced',[24] for instance, seems evident in *The Living And The Dead*, offering the only alternative to the miserable which envelopes its characters, a glimpse of plenitude and permanence in an aesthetic world complete in itself and exempt from 'the singular, feverish sense of waste' (185) running through their lives, swept along as they are by the maelstrom of history.

---

23. Patrick White, *Happy Valley* (London: Harrap, 1939), 140.
24. EM Forster, "Art For Art's Sake", *Two Cheers For Democracy,* 101.

The clearest example of this release is Elyot's boyhood experience on holiday at Ard's Bay:

> It was an almost enclosed, almost circular bay. He spent many hours looking into pools. There were crabs. There were red, blunt anemones and the paler, trailing kind. He took up the smooth stones in his hand, the red and mauve stones, that shone when you took them out of the water. And standing on the rim of the bay, holding the rounded stones in his hand, everything felt secure . . . You looked into water and saw the shape of things (101–102).

True, the release it offers is only temporary here and elsewhere in the novel. But it is the kind of experience which was to become crucial in White's subsequent work and indeed its goal, since in it, as Hurtle Duffield, the artist hero of *The Vivisector*, described it, 'dreams and facts . . . [are] locked in an architecture which did not appear alterable',[25] and meaning, perception and being are somehow united so that it witnesses to the 'hope, wrested from reality by negating it' which Adorno saw as 'the only form in which truth appears'[26] and offers an alternative to 'the unspeakable world that is'.[27]

It is from this position, I suggest, that White's subsequent preoccupation with metaphysical and, indeed, theological issues developed, and Albert Solomon's understanding of the way in which Walter Benjamin's thinking developed from an aesthetic of this kind to a theological position illuminates this development. As Solomon sees it, it was Benjamin's 'experience of the human lot as a communion of suffering' which gradually convinced him that that 'the totality of the Condition Humaine is only intelligible to theological categories'[28] since they alone offered release from 'the catastrophic phenomena of history', an epistemological leap which would 'lift a historical period or event out of the continuum of history'.[29] Similarly in White's later work suffering seems to be a precondition for vision.

---

25. Patrick White, *The Vivisector* (London: Cape, 1970), 217.
26. Theodor Adorno, *Minima Moralia: Reflections From A Damaged Life*, translated EFN Jephcott. (London: New Left Books, 1994), 98
27. Kaufmann, *The Portable Nietzsche*, 41.
28. Bram Mertens, Hope, Yes, But Not For Us: Messianism And Redemption In The Work Of Walter Benjamin', in *Cross Currents*, 53/4 (Winter 2004): 63.
29. Mertens, Hope, Yes, But Not For Us: Messianism And Redemption, 72.

To return to *The Living And The Dead*, it could therefore be said that Elyot's experience at Ard's Bay and others of the same kind did not enable him to make this kind of leap since they remained at the aesthetic level only and failed to move to the ethical and thence to the theological, with the result that his story ends more or less where it began, imprisoned, with no sense of direction or obligation. There is no time here for detailed exploration of the way White's own thinking developed from this purely aesthetic position, only to point briefly to stages along the way as he interrogates more strenuously the world of commonsense and looks to ways of negating it.

His next novel, *The Aunt's Story*, written as he was thinking of returning to Australia and published in the year of his return 1948, turns away from the historical time in which *The Living And The Dead* is situated to the polysemous time of myth—the Modernist manoeuvre practiced by Eliot and Joyce and in a slightly different way by Lawrence. Theodora Goodman, the novel's protagonist, is a Ulysses figure, attempting to find her way home to the Ithaca of her childhood experience of the 'gnarled aboriginal landscape' of Meroe, which is the name of the fabled capital of ancient Abyssinia but also of the family station on which Theodora grows up. Her goal is to return to what she experienced there, the state WH Auden described as

> . . . the pact with pure feeling,
> The flesh as it felt before sex was,
> Archaic calm without culture or sin.[30]

But it is not so much a place as a state of mind since she arrives there not in Australia but in a deserted house in the Rocky Mountains in USA where 'there were no clocks. There was a time of light and darkness. A time of crumbling hills. A time of leaf, still, trembling, fallen.'[31] Nevertheless it could be said that she remains merely at the aesthetic level, having reached only 'the solitary land of the individual experience, in which no fellow footfall is ever heard' celebrated in the novel's epigraph.

The change comes, however, in the next novel, *The Tree Of Man*. Its protagonist, Stan Parker is an Australian everyman who sets out as a pioneer into the bush, takes up land, marries and has a family,

---

30. Patrick White, *The Aunt's Story*. (London: Eyre & Spottiswoode, 1969), 19
31. WH Auden, *The Age Of Anxiety* (London: Faber & Faber, 1948), 16–17.

goes to war and returns, battles floods and fires and the struggles to make ends meet and learn to come to terms with disappointment. Outwardly he seems to achieve very little. But inwardly even in the apparently hollow spaces of an ordinary life he is able 'to see around the corner, where different, unfamiliar life may be going on', which is at the centre of Ernst Bloch's *The Principle Of Hope* sensing a richness, sensing at times in 'the touch of hands, the lifting of a silence, the sudden shape of a tree or presence of a first star . . . [a hint of] eventual release'.[32] But this experience is not solitary but a release into community, into the recognition that comes to him at the end of his life that 'One, and no other figure is the answer to all sums' and that he is part of a 'large triumphal scheme'[33] beyond the divisions of history and society.

This recognition that, as Hurtle Duffield's comes to understand in *The Vivisector* 'he was not his own dynamo'[34] marks a crucial point in White's development, at least if we take the point Levinas makes that it is 'in the laying down by the ego of its sovereignty . . . that we find ethics and also very probably the spirituality of the soul, but most certainly the question of the meaning of being, that is, its appeal for justification'.[35] This brings into play the dialectic between self and other which is largely absent from White's earlier work and also the sense of responsibility for the other it entails and makes for an active questioning of the justice of the present order and giving it a theological colouring in the next novel *Voss* and even more explicitly in *Riders In The Chariot*.

In this novel the symbol of the chariot which dominates the novel and holds the four central characters together is explicitly theological since it is the Biblical symbol of divine power which the prophet Ezechiel describes leaving the temple as punishment for Israel's infidelities and thus implies a similar judgement to the citizens of Sarsaparilla, White's mythical Sydney suburb. But the vision of the chariot given to the four central characters, the riders in the chariot, enables them to see beyond the maelstrom of history which Heinrich Blucher[36] believed to be leading 'from humanity to nationality to

---

32. Patrick White, *The Tree of Man*. (Ringwood Vic: Penguin Books, 1963), 49
33. White, *The Tree of Man*, 477.
34. White, *The Vivisector*, 147.
35. Sean Hand, editor, *The Levinas Reader* (Oxford: Wiley Blackwell, 1993), 85.
36. Kohler and Saner, *Correspondence*, 278–279.

'bestiality' and producing a 'boiling mass of ghost-like individuals'— people like Mrs Flack and Mrs Jolley and the Rosenbaums, Jews who had renounced their Judaism.

From then on such people are constant targets for White not, however, for aesthetic reasons but because they have surrendered to history, and, in Blucher's words, have 'lost sight of eternity' and become 'the rout of men animals', 'swimming and sinking, trampling and being trampled . . . carried along' by the maelstrom.[37] In contrast the four riders, each in a different way apparent victim of history, Himmelfarb, a Jew escaped from the Holocaust, Alf Dubbo, an Aboriginal fringe dweller and gifted painter, Mrs Godbold, an Earth Mother figure married to a brutally uncomprehending husband, an Miss Hare, an eccentric spinster living in the ruins of her family mansion, all live more or less in their own inner space in which, to quote Bloch[38] again, a 'strange, inner dream work may go on and strike undisturbed' into the everyday, to offer an 'anticipatory illumination' of a further state beyond the 'thick darkness' of alienation and violence.

The estrangement from commonsense this involves, however, opens up a meaning that is never finalised offering liberation from the closure and imprisonment evident in the early novels and the possibility of a 'transvaluation of value'. It also offered a liberating 'deconstruction' of traditional ideas of God, uncoupling them from the 'the unspeakable world that is', showing it to be, as Nietzsche had argued, merely a 'surface and sign-world'[39] and the 'God' who presided over it to be its captive. Subsequent novels from *The Solid Mandala* on continued to explore the alternative to this 'surface' world, located it is true, as one of the epigraphs to that novel insists, 'in this one' but in its unexplored depths 'not outside . . . [but] inside: wholly within', as another epigraph, from the mystic, Master Eckhart declares.

White's achievement, then is the 'rescue of semblance', deepening the world we live in, by 'the promise of non-semblance'[40] even in the midst of history which makes existence liveable within it by halting its flow and contesting the direction it is taking and making human fulfilment possible in it, even or perhaps especially, for people like the

---

37. Kohler and Saner, 278–279.
38. Daly, *The Fate*, 84, 82.
39. Carl Rasche, 'The Deconstruction of God', in Thomas Altizer *et al*, editors, *Deconstruction And Theology* (New York: Cross Road, 1982), 6.
40. Patrick White, *Riders In The Chario* (Ringwood, Vic: Penguin Books, 1964), 120.

strange, eccentric and sometimes damaged characters he assembles in his novels. But he does this by enhancing the significance of their lives not just with aesthetic understanding but with the help of Benjamin's 'dwarf in the chess machine', the dwarf of theology, 'small and ugly nowadays, and [unable to] show itself under any circumstances' but able nevertheless to contest the dragon of historical materialism.[41]

---

41. Mertens, 'Hope', 69.

The Poetics Of Place:
Judith Wright's 'At Cooloola'

Let us begin by recalling and honouring the land on which we are gathered and the people who lived on and cared for it for thousands of years. This is not a sentimental gesture. DH Lawrence defined sentimentality as 'working off in words of feelings you haven't you haven't really got.' But we are concerned here with the reality of place and with our feelings for it, and the fact is that it has a history and that its First Peoples have since time immemorial been an essential part of it. To acknowledge them therefore is crucial to a proper understanding of it. I would argue therefore that our failure to do so in the past may be one of the reasons for the crisis in our relations with the land which is now facing us.

If I may elaborate further on this, this helps to explain why we need to develop what I call a 'poetics of place', a feeling for the land and for its First Peoples. Mircea Eliade, for instance, sees this, the 'transformation of chaos into cosmos', as the primary task of any people newly arrived in 'a place hitherto unknown to them'.[1] Yet by and large we have not been very successful in doing this. As Aboriginal leader Patrick Dodson observes; 'most Australians don't know how to think themselves into the country, into the land' whereas Aboriginal people 'find it hard to think without the land' (Keeffe, 2003, 35). The controversy over the short-listing for this year's Archibald Prize of an Aboriginal artist's self-portrait which was essentially a painting of the country in which she lived is an example of this difference.

In fact in the past and possibly still in the present it seems as if many of us feared the land. In the early years of settlement especially

---

1. Mircea Eliade, *The Myth of The Eternal Return: Or, Cosmos And History* (Princeton, Princeton University Press, 1974), 10.

there was much talk of 'conquering' it—conquest, after all, was the dominant concern of colonisation. The first settlers mostly saw the land as an empty container to be filled with animals, crops, towns and cities and so rendered 'productive'. It was, in Paul Carter's words, a kind of theatre in which 'Nature's painted curtains [were] drawn aside to reveal heroic man at his epic labour on the stage of history.' (Carter, 1987, xv) But it seems to me that ignoring the power of the land has held back the work which at this conference Peter Hay has argued is necessary for any would-be civilised community, the creation of a 'moral community', that is, of finding our place in the larger scheme of things, what Eliade calls the 'cosmos'.

The thinking of Emmanuel Levinas is relevant here. For him it is 'in the laying down by the ego of its sovereignty . . . that we find ethics and also probably the very spirituality of the soul, but most certainly the question of the meaning of being.'[2] What confronted us when we arrived in this country was an other-than-self, an environment very different from anything we had known on the other side of the world, a reminder that there are 'more things in heaven and earth than are dreamed of' in our Western culture that ultimately we are not in charge of the universe but that we are—to borrow this time from Martin Heidegger—'thrown' into existence as *Dasein,* the point at which Being (*Sein*) knows itself as there (*da*) and mortal and finite. This, as Levinas argues, is the beginning of a genuinely ethical existence which rests on responsibility

Self is not supreme; instead it is involved in and responsible to being as a whole. It follows therefore that settling in a new country is not so much a matter of exploiting it for our own human ends, *building on* it, as of learning to *dwell in* it, becoming part of a larger reality, what Heidegger calls, 'the fourfold' a relationship between 'earth and sky, divinities and mortals'.[3] Significantly, this is how Aboriginal peoples have always lived in and with this country, though by and large it is not typical of settler societies like ours. I want to argue, however, that it should be because what Stanner's Boyer Lectures in 1968 called the 'Great Silence' which has surrounded Aboriginal people and their culture and lead us to view the land and its history almost exclusively

---

2. Sean Hand, editor, *The Levinas Reader* (Oxford: Blackwell, 1993), 85.
3. Heidegger, Martin, 'Building Dwelling Thinking', in *Poetry, Language, Thought* (New York, Harper Colophon Books, 1975), 1.

from a 'white' perspective has excluded 'a whole quadrant' of reality from our understanding.[4]

But from the beginning one strain of our culture has attempted to explore and celebrate this area of reality, taking up the task of transforming 'chaos into cosmos'. This is the 'poetic' tradition, the area of the arts in general and of poetry in particular. concerned as it is with the dimension of the unconscious, of 'the archaic, the oneiric, the nocturnal' which, Paul Ricoeur argues, is accessible only by means of symbols, 'the surveyor's staff and guide for becoming oneself',[5] expressing what may otherwise be inexpressible, thus interrogating many of our cultural certainties and opening up new possibilities. This, I suggest, is happening in Judith Wright's poem 'At Cooloola' to which we now turn.

But first of all the poem needs to be put in context. Wright was born into a pastoral family who had lived on and by the land from the first half of the nineteenth century. Unusually, however, she was not entirely at ease with this colonial inheritance, and it was the land which was the source of this unease. As a child it was her constant companion: 'As a poet you have to imitate somebody,' she wrote, looking back, 'but since . . . I had a beautiful landscape outside that I was in so much and loved so much . . . it was my main subject from the start . . . It comes to me naturally' But it also became her teacher and the lessons it taught often were at odds with her culture's: 'Most children are brought up in the "I" tradition these days—the ego, it's me and what I think. But when you live in very close contact with a large and splendid landscape as I did you feel yourself a good deal smaller than just I.'[6]

It called, that is to say, for the ego to lay down its sovereignty, according to Levinas the source of ethics and of 'the very spirituality of the soul'.[7] So the land was not just a background to the self but an active force at work upon and within it, 'full of a deep and urgent meaning' which challenged the colonial culture to which she belonged: 'These hills and plains . . . these rivers and plants and

4. James Ley, '"How Small the Lights Of Home": Andrew Mc Gahan And The Politics Of Guilt', in *Australian Book Review,* 280, (April 2006): 37.

5. Paul Ricoeur, *The Symbolism of Evil* (Boston: Beacon Press, 1969), 348.

6. Veronica Brady, *South of My Days: A Biography of Judith Wright* (Sydney: Angus & Robertson, 1998), 469.

7. Hand, *The Levinas Reader,* 85.

animals . . . contained the hidden depths of a past beyond anything that cities and the British invasion had to offer.[8] Her loyalty lay there in the land, not in the glorification of settlement. So her much quoted poem 'Bullocky' which is often read as a celebration of the pioneering myth, actually presents him not as a hero but as a madman.

In her 'the hidden depths of the past' which she sensed in the land bespoke a presence which was also an absence for which she was somehow responsible. One of her early poems 'Bora Ring', for instance, a reflection on the remains of an Aboriginal ceremonial site, is about this presence:

> The hunter is gone: the spear
> is splintered underground; the painted bodies
> a dream the world breathed sleeping and forgot.
> The nomad feet are still.

But the responsibility remains. Their absence speaks 'an unsaid word', an accusation

> that fastens in the blood the ancient curse,
> the fear as old as Cain.[9]

In this world view we are all responsible for and to one another and to the land as living presence.

In this way she dissents from her inheritance. 'For A Pastoral Family' written in the 1980s reflects on the imperial assumptions of her forbears,

> . . . men and women
> who took over as if by right a century and a half
> in an ancient difficult bush. And after all
> the previous owners put up little fight,
> did not believe in ownership, and so were scarcely human

but finds in this inheritance an ambiguous 'base for poetry/a doubtful song that has a dying fall',[10] rejecting its implicit assumption that might equals right which therefore accepts the inevitability of

---

8. Judith Wright, *Going On Talking* (Sydney: Butterfly Books, 1992), 51.
9. Judith Wright, *Collected Poems: 1942–1985* (Sydney: Angus & Robertson, 1994), 8.
10. Wright, *Collected Poems: 1942–1985*, 406.

Aboriginal dispossession, the logic of the imperial history which has more or less obliterated the Aboriginal story which was exemplified by the judgement in the case of the Yorta Yorta people in Victoria, for instance, which argued that 'the tides of history' had flowed over their land and abolished any claim they might have had to it.

Wright's love for the land, however, took her beyond this kind of history to the time of the earth which had a different kind of story to tell. Another early poem, 'Nigger's Leap, New England',[11] is about this story. It is a meditation on a place not far from where she grew up where in the nineteenth century Aboriginal people were driven over a cliff in retribution for spearing some of the settlers' cattle. But the power of place interrogated her:

> Did we not know their blood [that] channelled our rivers,
> and the black dust our crops ate was their dust.

As far as the earth is concerned 'all men are one man at last' and those who died here are 'ourselves writ strange'. So

> . . . [w]e should have known
> the night that tided up the cliffs and hid them
> had the same question on its tongue for us.

This awareness contrasts with the ideological complacency which led one critic to write that the poem 'has for its subject . . . the suicide of the Aboriginals years ago.'[12] As the use of the adjective 'Aboriginals' rather the noun, 'Aborigines' suggests, he sees them collectively merely as part of a category different from his own and, as the word 'suicide' implies, somehow morally deficient. He is unable to think outside his ethnocentric frame and to acknowledge the claims of the other, an inability evident also in those who reject what they dismiss as 'the Black Armband school of history', the attempt to see things from the point of view of those excluded from official history.

Another poem, 'At Cooloola',[13] explores the link between Aboriginal people and the land and the ways in which white settlement interrupted it. But it also acknowledges her own involvement through her family

---

11. Wright, *Collected Poems: 1942–1985*, 15–16.
12. RF Brissenden, 'The Poetry of Judith Wright', in A V Thompson, *Critical Essays On Judith Wright* (Brisbane, Jacaranda Press, 1968), 42.
13. Wright, *Collected Poems: 1942–1985*, 140–141.

in this interruption, the way in which, as Levinas puts it, the '*da* of her *Dasein* 'has involved the 'usurpation of somebody else's place'.[14] Once again, this poem is a meditation on place which offers a challenge rather than consolation, a demand which she cannot fully meet but cannot avoid. It is set this time in a coastal area of Queensland, Cooloola, an area incidentally where clashes were later to occur between environmentalists and developers' intent on exploiting the mineral sands to be found here.

It is evening and the poet is watching a blue crane fishing in a pool. But once again we are drawn into the time of the earth in the realisation that the crane and his kind have been fishing in this pool 'longer than our centuries'. He is therefore 'the certain heir of lake and evening' and he will wear their colour till he dies'. But she is a mere onlooker, 'stranger, come of a conquering people.'

The sight of a piece of driftwood shaped like a spear thrust from the pool is a reminder of this, recalling an incident from her grandfather's diary, when one day riding at noon 'a black accoutred warrior armed for fighting' suddenly appeared before him and just as suddenly disappeared. In her family history, *The Generations of Men*, Wright associates this apparition with an incident some weeks earlier when he had come upon the bodies of three young Aboriginal warriors and one old man lying in the bush, evidently murdered. But he realised that they had been on a peaceful hunting trip since they were not wearing the feathers and clay decorations of men going to war. But they had been shot and dragged into the bush, and their bodies half-hidden by branches, perhaps the night before.[15] As the local justice of the peace it was his obligation to investigate. But in fact he had done nothing.

The implication in the poem, however, is that this apparition is a ghost representing the dead: according to his grand daughter the discovery had remained 'a heavy load' on his conscience. But for her the debt remains as she watches the crane:

> I cannot share his calm, who watch his lake,
> being unloved by all my eyes delight in,
> and made uneasy for an old murder's sake.

---

14. Hand, *The Levinas Reader*, 85.
15. Judith Wright, *Generations Of Men* (Melbourne: Oxford University Press, 1965), 50.

Ghosts, of course, have no place in current commonsense. But Aboriginal culture did, and still does: and the poem pays tribute to their beliefs:

> Those Aboriginal people who first named Cooloola
> knew that no land is lost or won by wars,
> for earth is spirit: the invader's feet will tangle
> in nets there and his blood be thinned by fears.

This is the crux of the poem but also of Wright's understanding of place. It is possible to dismiss this as merely 'poetic'. But many contemporary scientists, increasingly interested in and respectful of the unseen, suggest that the universe may be more open, subtle and supple than we have imagined,[16] and some would even regard the cosmos as a *'psychophysical* entity' evolving towards increasing consciousness, 'in this way both [producing] us and, ultimately, [participating] in us to become real'.[17] If this is so the poetic imagination may be more illuminating than common-sense.

Wright was aware of this, writing to a friend that 'even scientists . . . [no] longer regard the physical and the psychic as separate, and all the work being done seems to confirm this—what is the observer, what the observed? Can you tell the dancer from the dance?'[18] It may therefore true to say, that, as Heidegger put it,

> The oldest of the old follows behind
> us in our thinking and yet it
> comes to meet us in our thinking (Heidegger, 1975, 10)

and that the land may therefore be haunted. The fear expressed in 'At Cooloola' may be justified, not only existentially but also ethically. The fear occasioned by the death of these others, Levinas suggests, may represent not 'an *individual's* taking fright'[19] but the beginning of genuine moral community since as he argues, ethics can be seen as answer to what is said by the other—the other and the land being two sides of the one reality here.

---

16. Lyndon Harris, 'Divine Action: An Interview with John Polkinghorne', in *Cross Currents,* 48/1 (Spring, 1998): 3-14, here at 9.
17. James Studer, 'Consciousness and Reality: Our Entry Into Creation', in *Cross Currents,* 48/1, (Spring, 1998): 15–33, here at 21–22.
18. Brady, *South Of My Days,* 287.
19. Hand, *The Levinas Reader,* 84.

If this is so 'At Cooloola' may have important things to say about the problems facing us at the moment in the attempt to build and preserve 'moral community', to contest what Hannah Arendt calls the catastrophic interiority of the selfish *I*[20] by the 'laying down the ego of its sovereignty'.[21] To think oneself into the country may therefore be to think oneself into the meaning of being, to 'return to the interiority of non-intentional consciousness . . . to its capacity to fear injustice more than death . . . and to prefer that which justifies being over that which assures it.'[22] That, the penultimate stanza of 'At Cooloola' suggests, remains a task yet to be completed by us in this country. But the land itself keeps it before us:

> White shores of sand, plumed reed and paperbark,
> clear heavenly levels frequented by crane and swan—
> I know that we are justified only by love,
> but, oppressed by arrogant guilt, have room for none.

---

20. Julia Kristeva, *Hannah Arendt: Life Is A Narrative* (Toronto: University of Toronto Press, 2001), 39.
21. Hand, *The Levinas Reader*, 85.
22. Hand, *The Levinas Reader*, 85.

The Question Of Dignity:
Doubts And Loves And A Whisper From Where
The Ruined House Once Stood

From the place where we are right
flowers will never grow
in the spring.

The place where we are right
is hard and trampled
like a yard.

But doubts and loves
dig up the world
like a mole, a plough.
And a whisper will be heard in the place
where the ruined house once stood.[1]

(Yehudi Amichai)

The Oxford Dictionary defines dignity as 'a quality of being worthy or honourable; worthiness, worth . . . of high estate, position, or estimation, rank; nobility or befitting elevation of aspect, manner, or style; becoming or fit stateliness, gravity'. It even sets it in a cosmic dimension as astronomy defines it as the 'situation of a planet in which its influence is heightened by its position in the zodiac or by its aspects with other planets.' In this definition it is a concept associated with a world view which is at odds with what Edward Gibbon called 'the reigning deities of the age'[2] since its scope is cosmological rather

---

1. Quoted as the epigraph to Richard Holloway's *Doubts And Loves: What Is Left Of Christianity* (Edinburgh: Canongate, 2002).
2. Quoted in Czeslaw Milosz, *The Captive Mind*, translated from the Polish by Jane Zielonko. (Ringwood, Vic: Penguin, 1980), 198.

than individual, has overtones which could be dismissed as feudal, is certainly unfashionable and could therefore be said to be a whisper from the place where a ruined house once stood.

I would argue, however, that this whisper may have important things to say to us in the times in which we live which may still be said to resemble the culture which that shrewd observer Alexis de Tocqueville saw coming into the new United States of America in the 1830s. Its inhabitants, he wrote,

> owe nothing to anyone, they expect nothing from anyone; they acquire the habit of always considering themselves standing alone and are apt to think they have their whole destiny in their own hands . . . This [not only makes them] forget their ancestors but it hides their descendants and separates them from their contemporaries, throwing them back forever upon themselves alone and threatening to confine them entirely within the solitude of their own hearts.[3]

It is not a culture with much respect for the dignity of those who fail to achieve power or accumulate possessions, are physically, intellectually or emotionally disabled, or suffer from illness or fail to measure up to the norm. But I suggest that this earlier world view, still current in other cultures especially those of indigenous peoples, being less focussed on the individual as an end in and for her/himself has much to offer to us resting as it does on what Bourdieu has called 'symbolic capital, the accumulation of being', rather than 'having'.

This kind of capital is available to anyone, regardless of circumstance or social position and presumes that dignity rests on the assumption that every person has a valuable part to play as part of a larger order of things beyond the self and its interests. It also has a more expansive sense of value, implying that this order and every part of it is sacred since this assumption rests on the belief that, in the words of William James, 'the so-called order of nature which constitutes this world's experience, is only one portion of the total universe . . . and . . . [that] there stretches beyond this visible world an unseen world of which we know nothing positive, but in its relation

---

3. Alexis de Tocqueville, *Democracy In America*, edited and abridged by Richard Heffner (New York: Mentor Books, Times Mirror, 1956), 194

to which the true significance [and thus, I would add, the dignity] of our present mundane life consists.'[4]

This is the notion of dignity which Patrick White explores in his novel *The Tree Of Man,* the story of a very ordinary Australian man many people would regard as totally insignificant but the ideal figure of humanity White drew for himself in an attempt to preserve a sense of his own integrity when he returned to Australia in 1948 after many years overseas and service in World War II. looking for the state of silence, simplicity and humility' which he saw as the 'only proper state' for a human being,[5] but despairing of finding it in the ruins of Europe, an 'aching wilderness in which the ghosts of Homer, St Paul and Tolstoy sat waiting for the crash.'[6]

But the place to which he returned seemed like one described in Amichai's poem, 'hard and trampled/ like a yard.' Here, he wrote angrily, it seemed as if 'the mind was the least of the possessions . . . the rich man was the important man' and people were preoccupied with crude material pleasures whereas he had been longing to hear the 'whisper' which had come to him as a child from the land itself. In Stan Parker, however, he created a character who had nothing to do with these values and was in tune with the natural world around him and able to discover in it 'the extraordinary beyond the ordinary, the mystery and poetry which alone could make life bearable'.[7] Incidentally also, as he told John Hetherington, he hoped in this way to help the 'people of a half-savage country to become a race possessed of understanding.'[8]

For these reasons it may be useful to explore what this novel has to say about the question of human dignity. But it is also worth pointing out that in effect White was carrying on the task which Mircea Eliade saw as essential for any people if they were to settle properly into a place hitherto unknown to them, the 'transformation of chaos into cosmos'.[9] This transformation, I suggest, may well be

---

4. William James, *Varieties Of Religious Experience* (New York: Random House Modern Library, 1957), 51.

5. Patrick White, 'The Prodigal Son', *Australian Letters,* I, 1, 15–16.

6. Patrick White, *The Aunt's Story* (London: Eyre & Spottiswoode, 1948), 146.

7. White, 'The Prodigal Son', 15.

8. John Hetherington, *Forty Two Faces* (Melbourne: Cheshire, 1962), 140.

9. Mircea Eliade, *The Myth Of The Eternal Return: Or Cosmos And History* (Princeton: Princeton University Press, 1974), 10.

necessary if people are to become capable of the essential dignity, as the Dictionary defines it, which comes from knowing one's place in a larger scheme of things.

The title of the novel, *The Tree Of Man,* points to this larger order, echoing the mythical image of the universe as a great cosmic tree, a notion which many of the Romantics drew on. In his description of crossing Alps in Book VI of *The Prelude,* for instance, Wordsworth uses it with dramatic effect:

> The rocks that muttered close upon our ears,
> Black drizzling crags that spake by the wayside
> As if a voice were in them, the sick sight
> And giddy prospect of the raving stream,
> The unfettered clouds and region of the Heavens,
> Tumult and peace were all like workings of one mind, the features
> Of the same face, blossoms upon one tree:
> Characters of the great Apocalypse,
> The types and symbols of eternity,
> Of first and last, and midst, and without end.[10]

In this perspective everyone and everything becomes significant, even someone like Stan Parker who is in his own estimation and that of others 'nothing much', the son of a mother who 'read a lot'.[11] Stan's story is typical of many of his generation, outwardly in no way special. As a young man he sets out into the bush, clears a small farm for himself, marries, has children, battles floods, fire and drought, goes off to war in France, survives and returns to the farm. Outwardly as he grows older his life seems to diminish. The two children leave home and drift away, the city expands outwards and finally engulfs their farm and he and Amy, his wife, jog along together in mutual loneliness until Stan dies, with little apparently to show for his life. Yet, as we will see, the novel tells us that 'in the end there was no end' (480). What then is the source of his dignity?

It is not social. His neighbours pay little attention to him since he is not particularly sociable and to some he seems to have 'gone

---

10. In MH Abrams *et al*, editors, *The Norton Anthology Of English Literature, II.* (New York: Norton, 1962), 154–155.
11. Patrick White, *The Tree Of Man* (Ringwood: Penguin Books, 1963), 12. Henceforth all page references will be given in my text.

a bit queer from the war . . . [and] began to avoid him' as there is
something in him which makes them uneasy: 'He had never been a
talkative man, except on direct practical matters. His advice had been
good. But they preferred to take their troubles elsewhere, rather than
have his eyes discover any cracks in their demeanour. Stan Parker
was queer.' (221) What makes him 'queer', I suggest, is that his centre
of gravity lies within. He does not seem interested in the opinion of
others or in 'getting on'—and this, to refer once more to our original
definition of 'dignity', gives a him a kind of stateliness or at least a
deep confidence as the goals of his life are uncommon but also seem
somehow ordained.

His mother had insisted that he be called 'Stanley'—the name of
the famous African explorer and throughout his life he lives up to
that name. But the continent he explores is not physical but psychic,
the 'omnipotence of distance' (27) he senses within himself. Here
he is able to discover 'the extraordinary behind the ordinary, the
mystery and poetry' of existence which White himself was looking
for. As the epigraph to one of White's later novels, *The Solid Mandala*
puts it, for him 'There [was] another world, and it is in this one.'
In effect he is searching for the sacred, the mystery which fills us
with awe but also draws us to it, the order which William James
believed gives life its true significance. This, of course, does accord
with the kind of world view de Tocqueville described since it is not
so much concerned with 'getting on' or of making or remaking the
visible world to one's own ends but of knowing one's place within
this invisible one and behaving accordingly. Ultimately, it assumes
a sense of reality which is cosmological and even ceremonial. That
this is where Stan belongs and values is clear in the scene in which
a traveller recently returned from Africa visits him and Amy and
regales them with 'images of gold and ebony'. Stan is not drawn to
them, however. His Africa lies here:

> He did not wish to take his hat from the peg and say, Well, so
> long, I'm off to see foreign places . . . He had a subtler longing.
> It was as if the beauty of the world had risen in a sleep, in
> the crowded wooden room, and he could almost take it in his
> hands. All words that he had never expressed might suddenly
> be spoken. He had in him great words of love and beauty,
> below the surface, if they could be found (39).

But this is clear from the beginning of Stan's story. The description of him as he sets out into the bush echoes the *Book Of Genesis*, presenting Stan as an Adamic figure making his first impact on the world and naming it, taking his axe to a tree in order his place, 'the first time anything like this had happened in that part of the bush' (9). Then in the light of the fire he kindles this world begins to take shape, giving him 'the first warmth of content' but also making him aware of 'being there'. That particular part of the bush had been made his by the 'entwining fire' (9). One is reminded here of the image Heidegger uses to describe the work human consciousness has to do in shaping the world, comparing it to a fire lit in a forest at night which enables one to see that the tress are there. Similarly, the phrase 'being there' recalls his definition of the human state as *Dasein* (*da* being the German for 'there' and *sein* for 'being'), of being 'thrown into' existence, finite and mortal and being-towards-death—and, as we shall see later, Stan's death represents the culmination of his life.

This intuition that, as Shakespeare's Prospero says,

> . . . We are such stuff as dreams are made on
> And our little lives are rounded with a sleep,

remains with Stan throughout his life and the sense that it is also therefore risky, that, as White's next novel *Voss* says, 'the shelless oyster is not more vulnerable than man'.[12] This means that he never feels that life is humdrum. In fact inner events often matter more than external excitements. So, for instance, the climax of a violent storm which hits the farm, destroying sheds, felling trees and threatening stock, occurs not during it but in its aftermath as Stan calmly goes about his evening work:

> He was tired. He was also at peace under the orange sky, events had exhausted him. He had learned not to think fat, and in what progress he had made had reached the conclusion he was a prisoner in his human mind, as in the mystery of the natural world. Only sometimes the touch of hands, the lifting of a silence, the sudden shape of a tree or presence of the first star, hinted at eventual release (49).

---

12. Patrick White, *Voss* (Ringwood, Vic: Penguin, 1971), 349.

Identity for many people is a 'closed circle around sameness'[13] beyond which they are afraid to move and their dignity depends on recognition within it. But Stan has discovered that, in the words of Emmanuel Levinas 'it is in the laying down by the ego of its sovereignty . . . that we find ethics and probably also the very spirituality of the soul, but most certainly the question of the meaning of being.'[14] Stan has made this move from the beginning. As if to underline this and the significance of his name, we are told that his mother had originally thought she would call him Ebenezer (which means 'rock of deliverance) but changed it to Stanley because 'she remembered the explorer' (10). His task, to draw on the comparison Heidegger makes, is not so much to *build on* the world but to learn to *dwell within* it,[15] a task which calls him to be continually moving beyond the 'closed circle around sameness.

He is at home with the 'doubts and loves/ [which] dog up the world' rather than the 'hard and trampled' yard of present commonsense. So the novel has almost nothing to say about Stan's time at war, dismissing it as a time of 'mud and metal' (199) or about Amy's passing infidelity with a commercial traveller or their children's gradual rejection of them. They have little to do with love or indeed the doubt which points beyond itself to the mystery of things. For him the 'whispers' he is listening for come from here, disturbing the world within the circle of accepted reality. To put it simply, he lives less by matter-of-fact than by the kind of imagination Keats compared to 'Adam's dream—he awoke and found it truth'.[16] In a way this enables him to rehearse his life and even his death. Towards the end, for instance, he and Amy go to see *Hamlet*, and in it, watching Hamlet leap 'radiantly into the presence of death' and realising that 'the end of Hamlet is too complicated to follow unless lived' (405), he accepts that he too is about to die.

As it is presented, however, this death is the climax of his story and his final achievement. It is winter-time and Stan, now old and frail, is sitting in the weak sunshine in the overgrown garden, which is all that is left of their farm. But far from a sense of failure he is feels himself 'large, triumphal scheme' and seated at the heart of it:

---

13. Luiz Carlos Susin, 'A Critique Of The Identity Paradigm', in *Concilium*, 2 (2002): 88.
14. Sean Hand, editor, *The Levinas Reader* (Oxford: Blackwell, 1993), 85.
15. Martin Heidegger, 'Building Dwelling Thinking', in his *Poetry, Language, Thought* (New York: Harper Colophon Books, 1975), 143-162
16. Abrams *et al*, *The Norton Anthology of English Literature I*, 396.

> From this heart the trees radiated, with grave movements
> of life, and beyond them the sweep of a vegetable garden .
> . . All was circumference to the centre, and beyond that the
> worlds of other circles, whether crescent of purple villas or the
> bare patches of earth . . . The last circle but one was the cold
> and golden bowl of winter, enclosing all that was visible and
> material (474).

Though it is much more peaceful, there are echoes here of Wordsworth's vision, quoted earlier, of the 'great Apocalypse' in which all things appear as 'types and symbols of eternity'. But just at this moment a young man, the embodiment of the individual's will to power, a self-appointed evangelist, absorbed in himself hurdles the garden fence and comes towards Stan, 'stepping over beds rather than following paths . . . convinced of achieving his mission by 'direct means and approaches'. Once there, he pours out before the old man the story of his life, presenting himself 'in the most complete nakedness' telling of 'drinking and whoring most weekends', reaching a triumphant conclusion when he describes his conversion when he fell on his knees, and grace descended upon him' and then telling the old man that '"This can happen to you too"' (475).

But Stan has always suspected certainty, aware as he is that life is ultimately mysterious. So he thinks to himself that if this young man can understand this mystery, 'then it is a miracle' and replies mildly that he is 'not sure whether I am intended to be saved' (475). As the narrator remarks, however, 'no subtleties would escape the steam-roller' of the young man's faith who babbles on, offering to 'show you books' about God. Stan now feels that he has 'been cornered enough' and spitting on the ground points with his stick at the gob of spittle 'as it lay glittering intensely and personally on the ground', "That is God," he said' (476). This puts the evangelist to flight, leaving Stan alone to his contemplation as 'a great tenderness of understanding rose up in his chest. Even the most obscure, the most sickening incidents of his life were clear in that light.' (476) as he understands that 'One, and no other figure, is the answer to all sums' (477).

As William Blake insisted; 'Everything that lives is holy', part of one great pattern, even disappointment and failure, death and disease. As if to affirm this belief, as he gets up to go indoors, he stabs with his stick at a leaf lying on the path, saying '"I believe in this leaf."' But then he is overtaken by a fit of trembling and stands still 'waiting for the flesh to be loosened on him' (477). Then he collapses and dies. But the novel tells us that his story does not end here. The epilogue returns to the beginning of the story with Stan's grandson walking through the trees and deciding that he will write a poem about life, of all life, of what he did not know, but knew' and thus take up his grandfather's work, aware as he was, of a 'greatness' within him, even if it was still his secret (480).

To conclude then. White presents a picture of dignity which has nothing to do with social position, wealth or external achievement but consists in knowing one's place in the universe, accepting it and living it to the full, independent of the judgements of others. This is also true of other characters in the novel, notably Amy's friend, the rumbustious Irishwoman Mrs O'Dowd. Married to a man who 'goes mad and violent with the drink', she manages in her own way to cope and to care for him and others and when she is diagnosed with cancer remarks philosophically, '"I know it is intended that way"', declaring at the same time that she '"will give it a tussle as it always has been."' The contrast White draws between her and Amy at this moment underlines the point that Mrs O'Dowd's dignity comes from her sense of a larger order of things beyond personal desire or need. So Amy protests against her friend's acceptance of death. 'Holding her own hands that had begun to tremble, for however much love and pity she did truly feel towards her friend, the experience of pain was also hers. She was aghast at her own unreliable relationship to life' (449) unreliable, it is implied, because she cannot accept this larger order.

In this way the novel accepts that as the Elizabethan divine Richard Hooker argued, 'the obedience of creatures unto the law of Nature is the stay of the whole world'.[17] Before him Dante expressed a similar view:

> The more there are who would say 'ours'
> so much the greater is the good possessed
> by each—so much the more love burns in that cloister.[18]

---

17. Abrams *et al*, *The Norton Anthology Of English Literature I*, 389.
18. Dante Alighieri, *The Divine Comedy*, translated by Allen Mandelbaum (New York: Bantam Books, 1984), *Purgatorio*, XV, lines 55–58.

This is not a fashionable view today. As we have suggested, Stan would not fit easily into our present society since there is little that is competitive or go-getting about him. But in his dealings with others he embodies this sense of community, mutual respect and readiness to care for others, regardless of their social position—as, for example, when he rescues Madeleine, a rich young woman, from her burning mansion significantly named 'Glasonbury', perhaps to indicate that as a shrine of wealth and power, it is destructive.

To conclude, then, I believe that this kind of dignity is the basis of a civilised society since it accords equal value to everyone, rich or poor, old or young, ill, healthy even deserving or undeserving. It also involves the kind of respect for the natural world which Stan embodies and his readiness to accept its mysterious power. As Paul Ricoeur observes: 'Cosmos and Psyche are the two poles of the same expressivity; I express myself in expressing the world; I explore my own sacrality in deciphering that of the world'[19] so that it helps him understand the meaning of existence.

Self-centredness, competition and greed lead to what Thomas Hobbes saw as the 'war of every man against every man.' Suffering and violence will always exist, it is true, and probably is built into the nature of things. But that means that we must learn to deal with it without allowing it to destroy our dignity as human beings and our trust in existence as a whole.

---

19. Paul Ricoeur, *The Symbolism of Evil* (Boston: Beacon Books, 1969), 12.

'But Play You Must . . . ' Problems of Attempting Religious Communication in Australia

Ours is said to be an age of communication. But the communication is *mass* communication and the means involved are electronic—not necessarily the best for communicating experiences of a religious kind at least if we define religion as 'commitment to realities at present unseen' (Heb 11:1), to the extent that, as Baudrillard says, mass media rest on 'the exaltation of *signs* based on the denial of the reality of *things*'[1]—and, I would add, of people. But our subject, religious communication, is the relationship between people and things and the ultimate THING, absolute reality and with enabling human beings to experience and respond to it.

So it is ultimately and perhaps uniquely individual—a journey of 'the alone to the Alone' (as John of the Cross puts it)—whereas the media creates and presupposes the kind of public domain Julia Kristeva describes which tends to diminish if not destroy the individual, generating 'a unanimous and mystical passion: that of the single man, and that of the people considered as a single man'.[2]

The religion which arises from this passion is the kind Marx attacked as the 'opium of the people', 'the generalised theory of this world, its encyclopaedic compendium', the product of human weakness and a projection of emotional, political or economic need. What we are concerned with, however, is a move in the opposite direction into the unknown, a 'still point of the turning world, neither

---

1. Jean Baudrillard, *Revenge Of The Crystal: Selected Writings Of The Modern Object And Its Destiny, 1968–1983* (Sydney: Pluto Press, 1990), 63.
2. Julia Kristeva, *Hannah Arendt Life Is A Narrative* (Toronto: University Of Toronto Press, 2001), 23.

flesh nor fleshless; / neither from nor towards,[3] which William James saw as an 'absolute addition to life' and Levinas as 'the true life', 'the normative idealism of what must be'.[4] Because it is so intimate, however, it is difficult to speak about.

This tension between modes of being and knowing is the subject of Wallace Stevens' poem, 'The Man With The Blue Guitar':

> They said, 'You have a blue guitar,
> You do not play things as they are.'
>
> The man replied, 'Things as they are
> Are changed upon the blue guitar.'
>
> And they said then, 'But play you must,
> A tune beyond us, yet ourselves.[5]

It is a tune 'of things exactly as they are', and the key word is 'exactly', a precision beyond us which is yet necessary if we are to be properly ourselves. This, of course, is what theology has traditionally claimed to do. But the poem points to the difficulty it faces in trying to speak about what is in fact 'an absence in reality', a *'mysterium tremendum et fascinans'* at the heart of existence which is unknowable yet speaks to us. Communicating this is an all but impossible task for philosophical and rational language, since what it is trying to express is 'total presence',[6] the sheer is-ness figured in the image of the bush burning but never consumed.

This kind of experiential presence in which, 'the visible becomes the visibility of the invisible',[7] I suggest calls for the suggestiveness of symbols at work in the 'blue guitar' of the arts. If or because official religious language fails us, then

3. TS Eliot, *Four Quartets* (London: Faber & Faber, 1954), 9.
4. Emmanuel Levinas, *Ethics And Infinity: Conversations With Philippe Nemo* (Pittsburg, Duquesne University Press, 2003), 21.
5. Wallace Stevens, *The Man with the Blue Guitar, and Other Poems* (New York: Alfred A Knopf, 1937), 52.
6. Carl Rasche, 'The Deconstruction Of God', in Thomas Altizer *et al*, Deconstruction and Theology (New York: Crossroad, 1982) 23.
7. Jean Luc Marion, *God Without Being* (London: University of Chicago Press, 1995), 23.

> . . . poetry
> Exceeding music must take the place
> Of empty heaven and its hymns.[8]

Let us take Paul Cox's film 'Man Of Flowers' as an example.

Significantly, it rejects the religion Marx attacked as merely the 'moral sanction' of the status quo.[9] (Easton & Guddat, 1967: 250) focussing instead on the experience of what Stevens calls the 'poetry exceeding music', which is identified here with both *eros* and *agape,* the 'Love which moves the sun and the other stars'. Its central character, Charles Bremer, is obsessed with his childhood vision of beauty in his brief glimpse of his mother's breast. To keep this vision alive he celebrates it once week at home in room filled with flowers in which a young women disrobes before him to reveal the beauty of her body.

The iconography here, the flowers and the mandala shape on the wall behind her—reminiscent of the monstrance in which the consecrated host is displayed in the ceremony of Benediction make this a sacred moment, agapeic rather than merely erotic, a vision of Augustine's 'Beauty ever ancient, ever new' but also of innocence, paradise regained. This is underlined by the fact that when she leaves, Bremer hurries across to the church over the road and as if to prolong his vision plays the organ so loudly that the vicar, coming in at that moment, remarks that the whole church is shaking, to which he replies, 'Yes, I know.'

Outwardly Bremer's life may be drab and solitary. But inwardly he is attuned to this 'exceeding music' which takes 'the place of empty heaven and its hymns', briefly transporting us beyond ourselves into a realm beyond metaphysics to experience a total presence, open infinity, the 'domain of sheer gift'[10] an 'absolute addition' to our lives, as James puts it.

My time is up. But I have been suggesting the 'blue guitar' of the arts may offer a way of communicating 'the primal saying of the sacred'[11] and its plenitude which is more powerful than we think.

---

8. Wallace Stevens, *The Man,* 54.
9. Lloyd Easton & Kurt Guddat (editors), *Writings Of The Young Marx On Philosophy And Society* (New York, Doubleday Anchor Book, 1967), 250.
10. Jean Luc Marion, *God Without,* xxi–xxii.
11. Max Myers, 'Toward What Is Religious Thinking Underway?', in Thomas Altizer *et al, Deconstruction And Theology* (New York, Crossroad Publishing, 1982), 130.

The Displaced Self Or The Displaced God?
Questions To Do With Freedom And Nature

We are reflecting here, I think, on a theological geometry which differs from Augustine's image of a circle whose circumference is everywhere and its centre nowhere. This triangle, 'God, Nature and Freedom', however, seems a shaky one today with its sides uneven and often contested, and in a society like ours what might seem the primary one, God, being most problematic and freedom probably the most popular. There are probably historical reasons for this. Traditional societies generally maintain a balance between the three. In them the first task of the individual is to his/her place in the world—which implies a link between God and Nature. But in a settler society like ours the task is rather to carve a place in the world for oneself. Freedom thus becomes central as the self seeks to impose its intentions on the world.

In this situation the fulfilment of these intentions becomes sacred, as Marx put it, becomes their 'spiritualistic point d'honneur, [their] enthusiasm, [their] moral sanction'.[1] As Charles Taylor describes it, this produces a 'buffered self' which is 'no longer open and porous and vulnerable to a world of spirits and powers', a 'disenchanted' self'.[2]

Theologically, but also, I would argue, psychologically and politically this is a problematic situation. But it is not, I think, inevitable. It is possible to balance the three sides of the triangle, and, assuming with Levinas, that literature may reveal 'the true life which

---

1. Lloyd Easton and Kurt Guddat, *Writings Of The Young Marx On Philosophy And Society.* (New York: Doubleday Anchor Books, 1967), 250.
2. Charles Taylor, *A Secular Age.* (Cambridge, Ma: The Belknap Press of Harvard University Press, 2007), 27.

is absent',[3] I suggest that Tim Winton's most recent novel, *Breath'*, may demonstrate how this accommodation may be achieved .

Its characters and setting are very ordinary; two boys, Bruce Pike, 'Pikelet', son of timid English migrants, and 'Loonie', the local tearaway, son of the local publican and an absent mother, who live in an isolated mill town not far from the coast of South-Western Australia. It is a dreary place, 'a closed circle around sameness'[4] from which the boys attempt to break out in a series of 'life threatening high jinks' which Pikelet later sees as 'a rebellion against the monotony of drawing breath' (5) and in effect gambling with death, The first of these involves a gamble with death, diving into the local swimming hole and holding their breath underwater so long that onlookers will think they have drowned. This is mere self-assertion. But Nature offers them a more splendid way out and a more heroic identity when one day they ride their bikes to the ocean and watching a group of surfers riding the waves catch a glimpse of power and beauty, some ultimate *mysterium tremendum et fascinans*—as Rudolph Otto's defines the sacred.

As Pikelet recalls it later:

> From the granite headland whose rocks were daubed with warnings about the dangerous current, the beach stretched east for miles. We watched the surfers plunged into a churning rip alongside the rocks and from there they shot out toward the break. Waves ground around the headland, line upon line of them, smooth and turquoise, reeling across the bar at the river-mouth, The air seethed with noise and salt; I was giddy with it.[5]

His narrow world is transformed as he realises that it is possible to 'do something beautiful. Something pointless and elegant, as though nobody saw or cared . . . as if dancing on water was the best and bravest thing a man could do' (23–24).

---

3. Emmanuel Levinas, *Ethics And Infinity, Conversations With Philippe Nemo*, translated by Richard Cohen (Pittsburg: Dusquene University Press, 1985), 21.

4. Luiz Carlos Susin, 'A Critique Of The Identity Paradigm', in *Concilium*, 2 ((2002): 78–90.

5. Tim Winton, *Breath* (Camberwell, Vic: Penguin/ Hamish Hamilton, 2008), 41. Hereafter references will be given in my text,

From then this experience is all the boys live for and they become disciples of the champion surfer Sando who involves them in more and more dangerous feats, surfing with a giant shark, for instance, or on reefs far from land, taken up into an ecstasy of freedom, danger and power centred on the self, they identify good and evil in a very particular way based on the way they way this experience makes them feel the 'basis and referent of the whole of reality [which seems] spread out at its feet'.[6] This is a self which, to quote Patrick White, is its 'own dynamo' as Nature becomes the equivalent of their God, making them superhuman, and beyond all restraint: As Sando declares exultantly: 'It's you and the sea. You and the planet . . . Man, it's like you've felt the hand of God. The rest of it's just sport 'n recreation. Give me the hand of God any day' (75–76).

Ultimately however, to draw on Kierkegaard's taxonomy, this experience is merely aesthetic and in the long run its intensity destroys Sando, his girlfriend, Eva, a former champion skier and Loonie who pursues his obsession with danger and power across the world to die in Mexico in a bar room brawl over a drug deal gone wrong. But. Pikelet survives since he eventually comes to recognise the claims of the other-than-self, of the ethical which Levinas suggests may open out into the theological. 'It is only in the laying down by the ego of its sovereignty [he writes] . . . that we find ethics, and also probably the very spirituality of the soul, but most certainly the question of the meaning of being, that is, its appeal for justification.'[7]

It is the other, it seems, which opens the way to this justification. From the beginning, inadequate as it may be, his family has reminded Pikelet of the existence of an order beyond self and thus of his own limits. In contrast, Loonie who recognises none is recklessly and defiantly fearless. But Pikelet fears the ocean's power and admits to it, even if for a time the its splendours outweigh the terrors he experiences there. Gradually, however, he returns to the centre as he begins to feel that 'maybe ordinary's not so bad' (198) and makes a choice to move to the centre away from self marrying, not very successfully it is true, but breaking up without acrimony, building an affectionate relationship with his daughters and making a career as an ambulance officer in which he 'saves lives and tries to be kind', thus finding 'a purpose in the world' (216) instead of attempting to escape from it.

---

6. Patrick White, *The Vivisector* (London: Cape, 1970), 147.
7. Sean Hand, *The Levinas Reader* (Oxford: Willey Blackwell, 1993), 85.

This may not seem to amount to much. But it could be said that he has achieved an accommodation between the three sides of the triangle, God, Nature and Freedom. The scene which opens the novel in fact is about this final accommodation. Now an older man and an ambulance officer, Pike is called to a death which the young man's parents think is a suicide. As Kierkegaard said, we live our lives forwards but understand them backwards. So remembering the way he and Loonie had rebelled 'against the monotony of drawing breath', he recognises what has happened. This young man had failed to pull out in time from the plastic bag over his head, had diced with death and lost. But now he understands what this means and where he belongs in the larger scheme of things and plays out this understanding on his return home.

Sitting still in uniform on he balcony of his empty flat Pike takes up the didgeridoo he learned to play years ago.

I blow until it burns. I blow at the brutalist condos that stand between me and the beach. I blow at the gulls eating pizza down in the car park and the wind goes through me in cycles, hot and droning and defiant. Hot as the pale sky. Hot as the flat, bright world outside. Once he and Loonie had rebelled against the act of taking breath asserting themselves against it. But now he is obedient to its rhythms, obedient larger than the self and its desires and finding peace in this submission.

Nature and freedom come together here. But God, the sacred, belongs here also—as the concluding scene makes clear. From time to time Pike tells us, he returns to where it all began. His parents are long dead and the town has changed, 'all wineries and bed-and-breakfast joints' (215). But the ocean remains and he is still transfigured by its power:

> I'm nearly fifty years old. I've got arthritis and a dud shoulder. But I can still maintain a bit of style. I slide down the long green walls into the bay to feel what I started out with, what I lost so quickly and for so long: the sweet momentum, the turning force underfoot, and those brief, rare moments of grace. I'm dancing, the way I saw the blokes dancing down the line forty years ago (215–216).

Perhaps WB Yeats provides the best gloss on this passage:

> An aged man is but a paltry thing,
> A tattered coat upon a stick, unless
> Soul clap its hands and sing, and louder sing
> For every tatter in its mortal dress.[8]

The 'buffered self' is broken open as soul claps its hands and sings. The sacred and the secular, obedience and desire are not antithetical but complementary. What Bonhoeffer calls a 'Beyond' can be found in the midst of our lives, a '*cantus firmus*' to which the other melodies of . . . life provide the counterpoint'.[9] Bruce Pike may seem ordinary enough. But from time to time his life is 'touched by those brief rare moments of grace' on the ocean. Out there he is free and 'never ashamed', still 'a man who dances . . . does something completely pointless and beautiful and in this at least . . . should know no explanation.

8.　WB Yeats, 'Sailing To Byzantium', in *The Collected Poems Of W B Yeats* (London: Macmillan, 1971), 217.

9.　Eberhard Bethge, editor, *Dietrich Bonhoeffer Letters & Papers From Prison* (New York: Simon & Schuster Touchstone Book, 1997), 303.

Religion, Division And Community:
A West Australian Case Study

AG Stephens, literary editor of *The Bulletin,* wrote in 1904 in the very early days of the new nation that 'the Australian environment is unfavourable to the growth of religion.[1] More recently Ian Turner offered socio-psychological reasons for this. The settlers were engaged in carving 'their own lives out of a remote and monstrously difficult wilderness; what they achieved they owed to themselves, and they found little for which to thank their fathers' heaven'.[2] By and large, this remains true today. But it gave rise to a model of identity implicitly based on the story of Ulysses who left home and travelled through strange places but always with the intention of returning home or making the strange places a replica of home, creating a community of sameness but also of coercion, a 'closed circle around sameness' with little respect for diversity.[3]

This describes the situation in the area we are concerned with in the wheat-belt in the mid-west of Western Australia. Once relatively prosperous, though marginal land, it has endured a series of droughts and now faces widespread salination and degradation of the land. So people have been defensive and there has been tension between local whites whose numbers and confidence are dwindling and it is obviously a community in need of regeneration. Perhaps surprisingly and certainly unfashionably, this is coming from a small group of Sisters from several Roman Catholic orders.

Why this is so can perhaps be explained if we reflect on the meaning of community. The Macquarie Dictionary defines it as 'a social group

---

1. Ian Turner, *The Australian Dream* (Melbourne, Vic: Sun Books, 1968), x.
2. Turner, *The Australian Dream, x.*
3. Luiz Carlos Susin, 'A Critique Of The Identity Paradigm', in *Concilium,* 2 ((2000): 87.

of any size whose members reside in a specific locality, share culture and have a cultural and historical heritage'. It is thus the product of imaginative as well as economic factors. Here the problem is the profound difference between the historical and cultural heritage of the Aborigines and the mainstream. Aboriginal people have lived in the area for thousands of years. But white settlers only arrived here in the late 1890s and the most rapid growth took place between 1905 and 1913—when respect for Aboriginal people and culture was minimal. As settler numbers grew Aborigines were increasingly marginalised, their children refused the education to enable them to cope socially and economically and when the Moore River Settlement, designed to destroy their culture, was founded in 1917 they were deported there.

So for a period, 'the natives' disappeared, 'gone between the defiled image and the indifferent gaze'.[4] But even before the Settlement closed in 1980 some Aboriginal people were drifting back to the area, not all of them the descendants of those who once lived here, so that they had little or no ancestral memory of the area and lacked its sanction--and even if they had it would have been seriously disrupted by their time at Moore River. As for the whites, as many farmers moved elsewhere and most of those who remained were preoccupied with the battle to survive economically and preserve their self-esteem and had little time or respect for the Aborigines, ghosts from a past most Australians want to forget, who had played little part in their ongoing battle with the land and were thus seen as 'bludgers', the opposite of the 'battlers' they believed they were.

Things began to change, however when the Sisters arrived. Initially they were supposed to work with the local priest they came in contact with Aboriginal women and children and wanted to do something for them—their faith making them aware that, as John Donne put it, no one is an island but we are all part of the one great continent of life. Where most of the whites were trapped in a 'closed circle around sameness', the Sisters were open to difference, seeing every human being as valuable and those who were poor and despised especially so.

Their goal was to help them to a sense of their own dignity, set them free to flourish as themselves but also to win respect and make a contribution to the local community. The former presbytery has

---

4. Rey Chow, *Writing Diaspora* (Indianapolis: Indiana University Press, 1993), 54.

become a Meeting Place where blacks can come together in town, and a community garden, an art project and a choir have been set up. A number of middle class white people are coming from Perth and even from interstate to celebrate and join in this work, raising the town's profile and making it a much less limited and fearful and more inclusive community in which people now share a common culture of work, but work in which people make themselves as well as earn money.

It may be then that religion of this kind has a significant contribution to building in this country.

A Forum for Theology in the World Vol 8 No 1&2/2021

So She Died as She had Lived, Moving Towards the End of her Life Peacefully

Dylan Thomas wrote a poem to his dying father begging him not to 'go gently' but to 'rage, rage, against the coming of the night'. But that was not the way Catherine Stack did it or would have wished to do it. She died as she had lived, gently and bravely, though it proved to be a longer and harder road she had to travel than any of us would have wished for her. So these last months have been harrowing for those of us who loved her—and no doubt for her, though she seldom showed it—as she waited for the Lord to come for her. But, of course, she believed that it was not the night Dylan Thomas spoke of but to bring her to fullness of life and to the loving-kindness of the God she had served so gently and faithfully.

Catherine was a Fremantle girl and proud of it but she was proud also of her Irish heritage. Both of her parents came from Kerry in the west, her mother from a little village on beautiful Dingle Bay and her father from Listowel further north past the Stack Mountains— was her father's surname 'Stack' connected? Certainly though when many years later with Sister Elizabeth O'Loughlin Catherine went back there, fulfilling a dream her mother was never able to realise, she loved it, though, typically, she 'felt guilty being there' when her mother never got back to Ireland, 'never. Nevertheless she felt that 'she'd be happy to know that I was finding my roots.'

Her father came to Fremantle in the early adventurous days before the wharf was built when ships had to anchor out beyond the reef and passengers were rowed ashore in small boats. But her mother arrived later with two of her sisters, coming to Australia more or less by mistake since their mother had intended them to go to America where her sister, their aunt, would look after them. But when they came to buy their tickets a man who had had to postpone his trip there persuaded them to buy his tickets to Australia for the much cheaper price he had paid to go to the USA. So Australia it was, though it seems that Catherine's mother had an unpleasant time of it, being sea-sick nearly all the way. Nor did things improve much when they arrived and desperately home-sick she decided there and then to save up and return home again.

But, like her daughter, it seems that she could not resist the impulse to care for others. When one of her sisters married and she and her husband were having trouble finding the money to buy a house, she gave them the money she had saved towards her fare back to Ireland. But not long after she herself married, having met her future husband at the home of his cousin where Kerry people used to gather after Sunday evening devotions. He was lessee a Hotel in Essex street but that was closed when the new Commonwealth Government decided that Fremantle had too many hotels. At first he looked for a country hotel to buy but found one for lease instead nearby in High Street and Catherine and her three brothers lived there. But when Catherine was fourteen her valiant mother who now had to support the family set out to manage a hotel at Bullfich in the gold fields. By all accounts she was a great success there, an American engineer remarking that the town was dead until Mother Stack arrived.

Looking back, Catherine remembered this as a 'terrible time, though she was happy at school and during holidays spent time with her father's brother Tom who had a beautiful seven acre property with the river on both sides and views of the city and King's Park. As she recalled it later, they used to pick wildflowers in spring-time in places there which are now shopping centres. After leaving school she worked in business for a year or so. But just before she turned 20, she made the long train journey across the Nullarbor to enter the novitiate in far away Ballarat, arriving on 11th February in drizzling rain and feeling the cold for the first time in her life.

It was wartime, everything was in short supply and her luggage had gone on to Melbourne. So her first days were more difficult than usual. There were only two postulants that year and the other, Pattie Waller did not stay. Years later, however, thanks to Sister Mary Murray, Sister Catherine met her again and even went to sat with her. But that first year, she remembered, was a lonely one. Indeed, moving around to different houses she often felt lonely, being professed and celebrating her various jubilees by herself. After her Profession, she was sent to South Melbourne to St Peter and Paul's school, to be trained by the formidable Mother Joseph who was disgusted by the little Catherine seemed to know of grammar--not a strong point, it seems, in West Australian schools in those days—then to Brisbane, in those days a kind of Loreto outpost where she stayed for 6 years, then back to Melbourne to Loreto Toorak, then back to Ballarat to Dawson Street and the next on to Adelaide. But in 1955 she returned home to Perth, to teach at Nedlands, welcomed back by her brothers Gerald and Jack who met her at the station.

But after twelve years in Perth where she was much loved by the little children she taught she was on the road again, to Ballarat to teach at Redan, the next year saw a surprise move back to Toorak and then back to Dawson Street the next year. In the meantime, however, Vatican II was bringing changes, which she welcomed—the old ways had not always been kind to her. When, for example, during the war her Air Force brother on his way overseas who had made his way from Melbourne to see her in Mary's Mount had nearly been turned away and had to fight to see her. Perhaps because of that she was open to change, though interested as she was in people she was always open-minded and spent a year as sub-Mistress of Novices soon after they moved to Normanhurst in Sydney and that was followed by a year at Assumption Institute in Melbourne which was set up in the aftermath of the Council.

After that in a sense Catherine came into her own. She had always been a loving and much loved primary teacher. But in the Blackburn parish school she became part of a Special Education project and in the parish community. Then, returning to Perth to Thornlie she and Sister Winifred Hubery were part of the parish and local community. When that house closed and she joined the Nedlands community she worked with the children and their parents at the new Mary Ward Centre for Special Education and when it moved to John XXIII she continued her work there and later after her retirement as a much-loved visitor. Then finally came the move to the Retirement Village at Success where, as usual, she was very much part of that community until the time came to move to the St John of God Villa in Subiaco where she was cared for devotedly until her death.

Having said all this, I realise also how much more there is to say—I have said nothing about her music, for instance, or of her gentle and thoughtful presence in the community, always ready to care for those of us who were 'busier' than she or of the courage and faith with which she responded to the many challenges of her life, especially in the days when some 'Superiors' seem to think that their task was to 'get tough', especially with humble and unobtrusive and members of the community. But even later on in life she seldom spoke about these things and simply got on with following her Lord and caring for others. It was in her final illness, however, that the simple heroism of her life shone out as she took whatever came, accepting the gradual diminishments her illness brought with it without complaint, continuing to be interested in and to support others in what they were doing and always grateful for visits and for whatever was being done for her.

So she died as she had lived, moving towards the end of her life peacefully, courageously and patiently, making no demands and accepting everything. And now she is taken up into the mystery of Resurrection. Reflecting on her life and death I think will increase our understanding of the mystery of it, especially perhaps of the way in which, as Paul says, what is 'sown in weakness' is 'raised up in power', into newness of life and the abiding mystery of the unconquerable Love that rules the universe. So let us welcome her entry into this life, grateful that her long time of waiting is over with this poem by a South American bishop, Pedro Casaldaliga

> And we shall, for all time, be ourselves
> as you are the One who, on our earth,
> was son of Mary and of Death,
> companion on all our journeys.
> We shall forever be what we are
> but most gloriously restored,
> just as those five wounds you bore
> are indescribably glorious.
> As you are the One who, human, brother,
> was just the same as the One who died,
> Jesus, the like and the totally other,
> so shall we, exactly, and for all time,
> be what we were and are and shall be,
> utterly other and yet ourselves quits.